LILLIAN (RICHARDSON) MARTIN

A Glimpse of a Life

Lillian Martin was interviewed by Tricia Smith of Legacy
Keepers on May 24th and May 31st, 2012.
www.legacykeepers.com

Preface:

I would like to begin by expressing my gratitude for those in my life who have made an impact on my life. When I started to write this book, I was going to name it "This is my story" as the song goes but my life has been blessed by so many I can't count and they are who I have become. My family: mother, father, brothers and sister, aunts and uncles and cousins. My friends: close ones, those that were in my life for a season: My forever friends and even those I didn't connect with taught me valuable lessons.

My extreme gratitude goes out to my special children: Theresa, Robert (Bubba), Scotty and Thomas. I always wanted children and this story tells in detail how I didn't have a clue how to raise children but I loved them and God protected and provided and taught us as we learned to trust Him. This book is for them. I hope they will see my heart as I explain what I have learned even after they have grown and out on their own. Our struggles were many and our blessings were many.

Please pass my love onto to my grandchildren and my great grandchildren and also to my special "grandchildren". Love will never end.

Me in 1948

Lillian Martin

I was told that my family on my mother's side came to America on the *St. Helena,* in 1678 and that it crashed on landing. Each of the seven survivors was given a thick piece of the wood taken from the ship and made into the shape of an iron used during that time. (It is a thick, one and half to two inch piece of wood in the shape of a traditional "flat iron". It is pointed at one end and squared off at the other with the date 1678 engraved on the "top" side.) It was handed down to my sister and she gave it to her son, David. The last name of the person on the *St. Helena* was *Mullen*.

There is supposed to be a museum on Pulpit Island off the coast of Castine, Maine that holds relics from this family.

My grandmother, Ella Mable Mullen was born in Castine, Maine. She was the first in her family to receive a high school diploma. That was quite an accomplishment in that time and for a woman. My Grandfather, William Erwin Connelly was born Scotland. They were married in Boston, Massachusetts. Their children and other information are included in their family tree.

My Grandmother, Ella Mae Mullin – was the first in her family to receive a high school diploma.

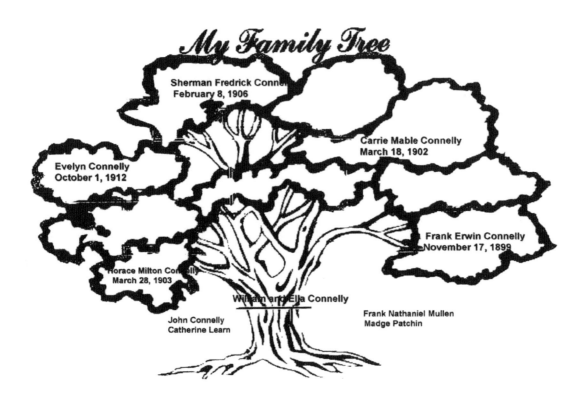

My Family Tree

Sherman Fredrick Conn[e]
February 8, 1906

Carrie Mable Connelly
March 18, 1902

Evelyn Connelly
October 1, 1912

Frank Erwin Connelly
November 17, 1899

Horace Milton Co[n]elly
March 28, 1903

William and Ella Connelly

John Connelly
Catherine Learn

Frank Nathaniel Mullen
Madge Patchin

I remember only two of my mother's siblings - Uncle Fred although his name was Sherman and Aunt Evelyn. I don't remember anything about the others. We (my brothers, sister and I) don't remember anything about our grandfather, William Connelly. He actually passed away six months before my aunt Evelyn was born. Obviously, that's why we don't remember him—he had passed away.

Husband: William Erwin Connelly (a.k.a. Connell)

Born:	1869	in: Scotland
Died:	March 18, 1912	in: Boston, MA
Married:	April 20, 1899	in: Boston, MA
Father:	John E. Connelly	
Mother:	Catherine Learn	

Wife:	Ella Mable Mullen	

Born:	September 18, 1881	in: Castine, ME
Died:	January 1, 1949	in: Billerica, MA
Father:	Frank Nathaniel Mullen	
Mother:	Madge Patchin	

CHILDREN:

1.	Name:	Frank Erwin Connelly	
	Born:	November 17, 1899	in: Boston, MA
M	Married:	March 11,1928	
	Died:	October 10, 1956	in: Billerica, MA
	Spouse:	Helen Betsy Smith	

2.	Name:	Carrie Mable Connelly	
	Born:	March 18, 1902	in: Dorchester, MA
F	Married:	April 2, 1921	in: Somerville, MA
	Died:	April 18, 1953	in: North Reading, MA
	Spouse:	Elwood Lyndon Richardson, Sr	

3.	Name:	Horace Milton Connelly	
	Born:	March 28, 1903	
M	Married:		

4.	Name:	Sherman Fredrick Connelly	
	Born:	February 8, 1906	in: Boston, MA
M	Died:	March 26, 1975	in: Boston, MA

5.	Name:	Evelyn F. Connelly	
	Born:	October 1, 1912	
F	Married:		

Died: February 21, 2000   in: Peabody, MA

Spouses: Jim Freestone, Leo Thibeault

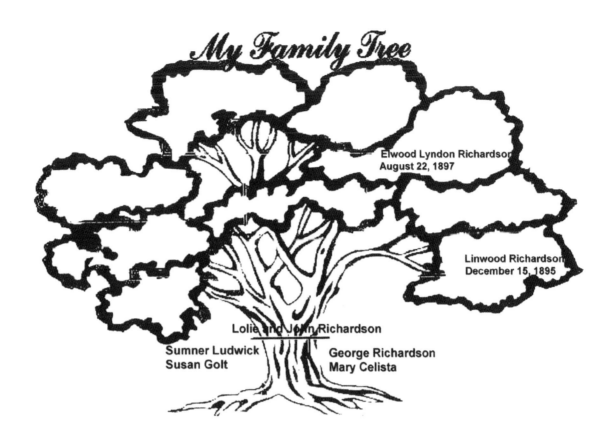

My Family Tree

Elwood Lyndon Richardson
August 22, 1897

Linwood Richardson
December 15, 1895

Lolie and John Richardson

Sumner Ludwick
Susan Golt

George Richardson
Mary Celista

My father's father, John Richardson, was a barrel maker. He had a shop of his own in Maine. My grandmother, Lolie A. Ludwick, and John Richardson were divorced, and by the time I came along, Gram had re-married Stanley Powell. I had a very hard time finding the marriage date for Lolie and John Richardson. They were married in Liberty, Maine September 7, 1895. I don't think my grandmother wanted that date to be known, but I found it. She didn't care too much for him at that time. In fact, he had to be buried in a different cemetery. He is buried in the Greeley Corner Cemetery in Liberty, Maine and she is buried in Sandy Hill Cemetery in Palermo, Maine.

Husband: John F. Richardson

Born:	February 15, 1870	in: Freedom, Maine
Died:	August 18, 1958	in: Tewksbury, MA
Married:	September 7, 1895	in: Liberty, Maine
Father:	George M. Richardson	
Mother:	Mary Celista	
Other spouse:	Rosetta Ridley (married February 15, 1913)	

Wife:	Lolie A. Ludwick	

Born:	September 4, 1875	in: Palermo, ME
Died:	September 30, 1966	in: Liberty, ME
Father:	Sumner Ludwick (a.k.a. Ludwig)	
Mother:	Susan Golt	
Other spouse:	Stanley Powell (married Dec 12, 1903 in Washington, ME)	

CHILDREN:

1. Name:	Linwood D. Richardson (a.k.a. Harry L. Richards, Harry L. Richardson*)	
Born:	December 15, 1895	in: Liberty, ME
M Married:	March 20, 1915	in Palermo, ME
Died:	March 21, 1981?	
Spouse:		
*marriage recorded as Harry L. Richardson		

2. Name:	Elwood Lyndon Richardson	
Born:	August 22, 1897	in: Liberty, ME
M Married:	April 2, 1921	in: Somerville, MA
Died:	September 9, 1956	in: Palermo, ME
Spouse:	Carrie Mable Connelly	
Other spouse:	Eva Flibotte (married August 3, 1953)	

I think Gram's second husband, Stanley Powell, had already passed away before I got into the picture. I don't remember anything about him. I think that I was kind of protected and not told very much, because I was the youngest of eight. I had to dig to find out what I found out later, when I was an adult trying to piece together the family history.

I spent a lot of summers at my grandmother's house in Maine. She had acres of blueberries and strawberries and a large farm, and each one of the grandchildren was expected to go every summer and help her with the strawberries and the blueberries. She was a great influence on me.

My mother had passed away when I was young, so I don't remember anything about her. Her name was Carrie, and she worked in a drug factory before she married my dad. My father, Elwood Richardson, worked for the railroad.

I was born at Winchester Hospital in Winchester, Massachusetts which is near North Reading Massachusetts, November 25, 1945 at 9:29 p.m. I weighed 7 lbs. 6 oz. and was 19 inches long. We lived on 129 Park Street in North Reading. I am told by my older brother, Billy, that my name was picked out from a storybook. My mother used to go to a Christian bookstore downtown in Boston and choose Christian books for everyone to read, and there was a character in one named Lillian. When my mother asked Billy, "Well, what are we going to name this one?" he said "Lillian," and that's how I got my name.

My mother was very close to Lillian Sergeant Bell. We called her "Aunt Lillian." My sister records that she was a niece to Frank Mullen, my mother's father – that should make one of his brothers or sisters her parent. I think that in addition to the name in the book, my mother wanted to honor her also. She was an accountant in Boston.

When I graduated from high school, Aunt Lillian took me shopping. She said I was to choose a watch that I would like. I chose one, and she said, "No, no—that's not expensive enough." She wanted me to have a real expensive watch. She had a lot of money compared to us, I think.

I don't think it was related to childbirth, but after I was born, my mother began getting sick. She already had a two-year-old—that would be Donald—and she was sick because of high blood pressure. They didn't have medication for blood pressure at that time. A couple from our church, Mr. and Mrs. Robert Anderson, took me in and watched over me because my mother couldn't do that.

The other kids were in school, and some were already working. I was over at Mrs. and Mr. Anderson's most of the time. The only thing I remember about my mother is her lying on the couch. I don't remember anything else. I was seven when she died. My brothers have told me more than I ever knew. My brother, Donald said something about she went into the bathroom and there was blood all over the place, and he didn't understand at all what that was. But all I personally remember of her is her lying on the couch. She died of Hypertensive Cardio Renal Vascular Disease.

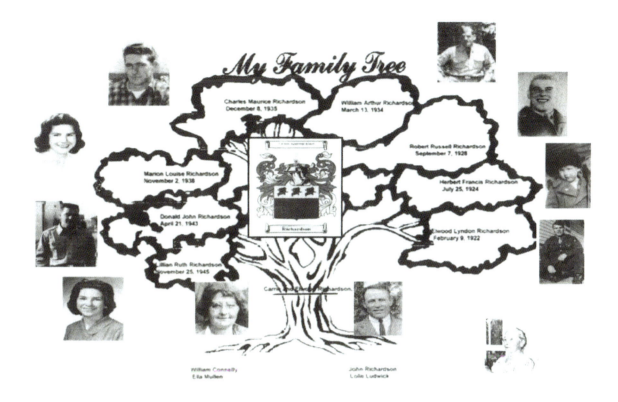

My Family Tree

Charles Maurice Richardson
December 8, 1935

William Arthur Richardson
March 13, 1934

Robert Russell Richardson
September 7, 1926

Marion Louise Richardson
November 2, 1938

Herbert Francis Richardson
July 25, 1924

Donald John Richardson
April 21, 1943

Elwood Lyndon Richardson
February 9, 1922

Lillian Ruth Richardson
November 25, 1945

Richardson

Carrie and Elwood Richardson

William Connolly
Etta Mullen

John Richardson
Lollie Ludwick

Wedding picture of my mom and dad

Husband: Elwood Lyndon Richardson, Sr.

Born:	August 22, 1898	in: Liberty, ME
Married:	April 2, 1921	in: Somerville, MA
Died:	September 9, 1956	in: Palermo, ME
Father:	John F. Richardson	
Mother:	Lolie Alice Ludwick	
Other Spouses:	Eva	

Wife: Carrie Mable Connelly

Born:	March 18, 1902	in: Dorchester, MA
Died:	April 18, 1953	in: North Reading, MA
Father:	William Erwin Connelly	
Mother:	Ella Mable Mullen	

CHILDREN

1. Name: Elwood Lyndon Richardson, Jr.

	Born:	February 9, 1922	in: Boston, MA
M	Married:	March 9, 1948	in: North Reading, MA
	Died:	January 6, 2010	in: Reading, MA
	Spouse:	Jean Elizabeth Tufts	

2. Name: Herbert Francis Richardson

	Born:	July 25, 1924	in: Somerville, MA
M	Died:	July 28, 1928	in: Somerville, MA

3. Name: Robert Russell Richardson

	Born:	September 7, 1928	in: Somerville, MA
M	Married:	ABT 1950	in: Toyko, Japan
	Died:	July 3, 1951	in: Korea

Spouse:	Chico Tanaka	

4.	Name:	William Arthur Richardson	
M	Born:	March 13, 1934	in: Somerville, MA
	Married:	June 2, 1958	in: North Reading, MA
	Died:		
	Spouses:	Janet Pettingill, Judith Dearborn Marshall	

5.	Name:	Charles Maurice Richardson	
	Born:	December 8, 1935	in: Somerville, MA
M	Married:	April 8, 1961	in: North Reading, MA
	Died:	September 8, 1973	in: Concord, NH
	Spouse:	Ruth Ann Fuller	

6.	Name:	Marion Louise Richardson	
F	Born:	November 2, 1938	in: Boston, MA
	Married:	March 25, 1958	in: Otis A.F.B. Barnstable, MA
	Died:	August 2, 2004	in: Appleton, WI
	Spouse:	Jimmy Alfred Wiersema, Sr.	

7.	Name:	Donald John Richards on	
M	Born:	April 21, 1943	in: Winchester, MA
	Married:	May 7, 1967	in: Reading, MA
	Died:		in:
	Spouse:	Maria Theresa Pellegrino	

8.	Name:	Lillian Ruth Richardson	
F	Born:	November 25, 1945	in: Winchester, MA
	Married:	November 19, 1964	in: Charleston, SC
	Died:		in:
	Spouse:	Robert Richard Martin	

I have seven siblings. My oldest brother, Junior, was born in 1922. His real name is Elwood, but we call him Junior. He was Elwood, Jr. after my father.

My brother, Herbert, was burnt in a fi re. They had candles back in that time, and Junior handed a candle to Herbert, and he handed it too close, and it caught Herbert's nightgown on fi re. He went to the hospital. I have a very moving letter from my mother that is very special to me, because I didn't know her, but this letter expresses her grief over what happened with Herbert in the hospital. It was also very special to see her handwriting. She was able to feed him a couple of times, but the doctor said it was not good, and that he would not live, and he did not.

Junior was very, very upset—that is clear from a letter that my mother wrote to my grandmother. I have both letters, because my grandmother saved them. My mother made the comment in that letter that Junior could not be comforted. In 2005 when I spent time with Junior, when I brought up Herbert, there were tears in Junior's eyes. Until the day he died, Junior felt responsible for his brother's death. I—and other members of the family— tried to tell him that was not true, but he did not believe it. He was very, very upset that he had done that.

My brother, Junior, was in World War II. He was hit by some shrapnel, and he got a Purple Heart. When he did come back from the war, even talking to his children, he didn't want to talk about it, and that's very common. But then his grandson, Michael Richardson, asked to interview him for a school paper. Junior gave him some information, and so we found out exactly how rough he had it when he fought in World War II.

deaden what pain there
was. She gave him a
heart stimulant but he
never responded to it at all.
The shock was so much more
than his heart could stand
When I think of him now
Oh Ma I don't know what
saved him from burning
to death in front of us here.
If he had come through his
mouth and neck would
have been disfigured. and
the place where the candle
fell on his chest was
burnt most through. It
was black. The whole
right side was burnt fierce.
I got home from work Sun.
morning about quarter of
eight and eight o'clock a
motorcycle officer was here
at the door and told us
to get to the hospital as
soon as possible. We
didn't stop to eat anything

(My oldest brother was named after dad, so he was called him Jr.)

World War II, My Grandfather's Experience, by Michael Richardson

My grandfather, Elwood Richardson, entered the war on September 26, 1942 when he was 20 years old. World War II began in 1939. The United States of America entered the war in 1941, when Japan attacked Pearl Harbor, Hawaii.

He left Boston Port in Massachusetts, and arrived in Cherbourg, France on September 15, 1944. His first battle was the Battle of the Zigfield Line, which was on the border of France and Germany, opposite of the Maginot Line. The Maginot line was in the north eastern part of France. It ran for about 200 miles. The Maginot Line was designed and built as a fortification to prevent frontal assault. The Germans invaded France in 1940 and flanked (bombed) the Maginot Line. He was there for 3 months shooting at the Germans in cement pillboxes, with a 240 mm cannon.

My grandfather was a tank commander. He was in charge of the 4 other men who were in his tank. The tanks were given orders to travel in front of the infantry to try to protect the soldiers. My grandfather made all of his crew learn how to work all the 5 positions in the tank, so that if someone were to be wounded or killed, the other men could fill that position. My grandfather lost 2 tanks by enemy fi re. On one occasion, a copy of 88 cannon shells shot through the tank. The shell had tracers (a device that shows you if you're shooting where you want to shoot). The cannon shells cut each of the other 4 people right in half. My grandfather was the only one to survive the attack. He had to pull the other 4 men from their positions in order to drive away from the first attack. The second tank was lost when the Allied Powers broke through the Zigfield Line, my grandfather's tank went right through a mine field and blew off one of the tank treads. They were tired from the battle and fell asleep. When they woke up they saw a Jeep flipped over with 2 soldiers dead. The Jeep drove over a mine near them and they were so tired, they never heard the explosion. Austin Lake, a foreign reporter, visited the accident site and wrote about this whole episode.

The conditions of the war were pretty rough. The food sources were served in either R rations or C rations. The meals were prepared in a box. They consisted of beans, soup, crackers, and cocoa. They would heat their meals up on the tank engines, and if the driver didn't have time to stop and take them off, the meals would explode, and would make a real big mess. They had to get supplies at night in order to be hidden from the enemy. A supply sergeant would come and give the men ammunition, fuel, clothes, and cigarettes. The soldiers couldn't shower, so they would take off their dirty clothes and put on clean clothes. The tank engines would get so hot that once my grandfather saw someone place their bare hands on the tank's engine and after he lifted his hands, there was no more skin on them.

A major battle that my grandfather was involved in was for the French city of Metz. He told me about another battle in the Hertigen Forest in Germany. The 94th Infantry were supposed to be fighting the Germans on foot, in addition to the tanks. The 94th Infantry left during the battle, and the tanks were not able to keep the Germans from climbing on the tanks. My grandfather and his tank mates had to prevent the Germans from entering the tanks by throwing grenades, and using machine guns.

My grandfather never met a famous general, but he did see George "Blood and Guts" Patton. Patton would ride in front of the tanks, and when the found a battle would return to get the tanks to lead.

My grandfather earned a Purple Heart, which is the oldest medal in the United States service. The first Purple Heart was awarded George Washington in 1782. It is awarded to members of the United States Armed Forces who have been killed or wounded in action against the enemy. It may also be awarded for maltreatment endured while a Prisoner of War. He earned his medal because he was shot through his left calf by a German sniper during battle. He also was wounded in his buttocks from shrapnel from a mortar shell while in his tank.

My grandfather was in Ulrichsberg, Austria on May 8, 1945, on V.E. Day (Victory in Europe). He traveled to Czechoslovakia, and then returned home to the United States. His battalion, the 778 Tank Battalion, was the third wave to arrive ashore, and the first tank wave to survive the war. They started in Europe with 155 enlisted men in his group. They had 302 replacements during the war to wounded or killed soldiers.

He retired his military career as Technical Sergeant, and received a Good Conduct Medal. The first thing he did when he arrived home after the war was to call his girlfriend to meet him with his car. He went to work as a boiler maker for the Boston and Maine Railroad. When I asked him about his memories of World War II, he said" there were good times, and bad times.

I am very proud of my grandfather, and what he did for our country during World War II, He was, and still is a hero. I never knew how interesting his life was until I interviewed him for this report.

My grandfather was injured before he went to Europe. He was participating in a "Black out March", which was a training where they would travel in the dark with the troops and trucks. My grandfather was a passenger in a truck carrying 5,000 gallons of gasoline in 5 gallon cans. The driver drove into a ravine by accident, and the truck tipped on its side. Luckily, the gas did not cause an explosion. He fell of top of the driver and had many injuries; he cracked one cervical vertebrate, cracked his scapular on his left shoulder, his left upper arm and his left lower leg. He was hospitalized for 7 months in Louisiana. My grandfather still feels discomfort from his injuries that he received during his time in the military.

Jean Richardson, Elwood's (Junior) wife was very special to me – even when they first were married in 1948, I was only 3 and we all lived in the same house. She told me I would come crawl into bed with them soaking wet and snuggle up to my brother, and say "My, Ju Ju". She was not upset with that – she loved me and I knew it. As I got older she would allow me to hang clothes out, clean dishes and play with their children (they had 7). I would wash dishes all Sunday afternoon until it was time to go to church at night. Other days I was there, I would hang out load of load of clothes on the line and when they were dry, I would bring them in and put them on Jr. and Jean's bed. I remember one day I was there when Jr. came home from work and saw all the clothes on the bed and said "I see you haven't got my playground ready yet." I was so embarrassed, I am sure he did that on purpose. She talked to me like she liked me – in fact I knew she loved me. She had a special kindness about her that was something so real that you wanted to be kind, too.

In March 1998, Elwood and Jean had a celebration of their 50th wedding anniversary.

She gave me a gift of a music box that played "In the Garden" which was the song I sang as my first solo at my grandmother's church. Jean did not know that. It was very special.

I remember one Sunday when I was staying with my grandmother, we went to her small church in Liberty, Maine, and when the pastor announced there was no special music for that day, my grandmother stood up and said, "My granddaughter will sing for you!" I sang "In the Garden" on that Sunday. So that has always been a very special song to me and for my sister-in-law to give it to me on her fiftieth wedding anniversary made it even more special. I still have that gift. I don't think Jean knew the connection, but it is very special to me. It connects the generations – my grandmother and my brother.

On their 50th wedding anniversary, I was escorted down the aisle by her oldest son, Johnny. Another expression of her love, since I was not able to walk down the aisle on their wedding day. The celebration was something she really enjoyed.

Very soon after the anniversary party, Jean was admitted to the hospital with an infection in her foot. She had diabetes. She died there suddenly.

July 9, 1998, Jean died of complications of diabetes and pneumonia and I made a trip to Massachusetts again. I had a chance to see each one of her grown children. It is so hard to lose your mom. My brothers and sister were there also to support my oldest brother's family and the loss we all felt.

_____

Me as flower girl with ring bearer at my brother's wedding

The music box Jean gave me at the 50th anniversary of their wedding

Because I hurt my eye, I couldn't walk down the aisle. Even so, they took a picture of me and the ring bearer. Jean always considered me the flower girl at her wedding.

Jean was the kindest person I ever knew. It's hard to explain how kind she was to everyone, everyone that she met. I remember when it was time for me to have my period and my stepmother wasn't into telling me anything about that, I mentioned that I'd heard from the kids that it was a pain, and I mentioned that to Jean. Even though she had seven kids of her own, Jean just took the time, and she sat down with me and said, "Do you want to have children when you grow up?" Of course my answer was yes—I watched her with seven. I said, "If this is what it's like, I want to have twelve." And she said, "Well, if you want to have children, then you have to go through this." And a simple statement like that was so encouraging to me. I didn't have anybody else to talk to about it, but Jean seemed to get right to the meat of it, and that's how it was. Jean died of complications of diabetes, twelve years before he did in 2010 – of Alzheimer's – where his mind basically told him not to eat. He expressed many times how much he missed his wife and wished to be with her. However, his seven children took very good care of him.

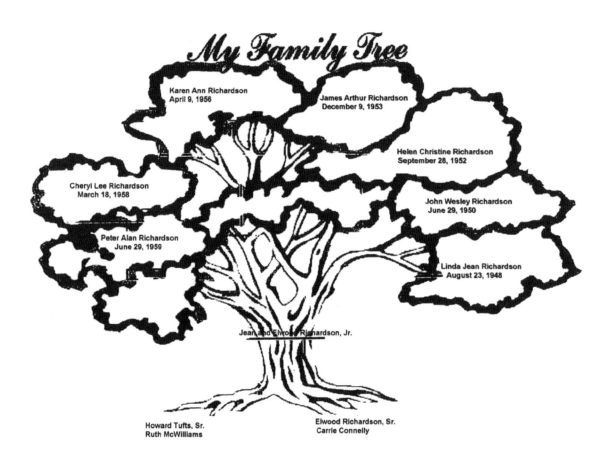

My Family Tree

Karen Ann Richardson
April 9, 1956

James Arthur Richardson
December 9, 1953

Helen Christine Richardson
September 28, 1952

Cheryl Lee Richardson
March 18, 1958

John Wesley Richardson
June 29, 1950

Peter Alan Richardson
June 29, 1959

Linda Jean Richardson
August 23, 1948

Jean and Elwood Richardson, Jr.

Howard Tufts, Sr.
Ruth McWilliams

Elwood Richardson, Sr.
Carrie Connelly

Husband: Elwood Lyndon Richardson, Jr.

Born:	February 9, 1922	in: Boston, MA
Married:	March 9, 1948	in: North Reading, MA
Died:	January 6, 2010	in: Reading, MA
Father:	Elwood Lyndon Richardson, Sr.	
Mother:	Carrie Mable Connelly	

Wife: Jean Elizabeth Tufts

Born:	May 5, 1929	in: Quincy, MA
Died:	July 9, 1998	in: Reading, MA
Father:	Howard L. Tufts. Sr.	
Mother:	Ruth Elizabeth McWilliams	

CHILDREN:

1. Name: Linda Jean Richardson

   Born: August 23, 1948   in: Somerville, MA

   F   Married: March 22, 1969   in: North Reading, MA

   Spouse: William Michael Rindone

---

2. Name: John Wesley Richardson

   Born: June 29, 1950   in: Somerville, MA

   M   Married: April 1, 1978   in: Reading, MA

   Spouse: Stephanie Marie Alicata

---

3. Name: Helen Christine Richardson

   Born: September 28, 1952   in: Melrose, MA

   F   Married: April 14, 1973   in: North Reading, MA

   Spouse: Robert David Pelley

---

4. Name: James Arthur Richardson

   Born: December 9, 1953   in: Melrose, MA

   M   Married: August 19, 1979   in: Reading, MA

   Spouse: Lisa Marie Winter

---

5. Name: Karen Ann Richardson

   Born: April 9, 1956   in: Melrose, MA

   F   Married: June 5, 1982   in: North Reading, MA

   Spouse: Frederic George MacKinnon

---

6. Name: Cheryl Lee

   Born: March 18, 1958   in: Melrose, MA

   F Married: May 22, 1993   in: NorthReading, MA

   Spouse: Anthony P. Brunetta

---

7. Name:	Peter Alan Richardson	
Died:	August 28, 2009	in: New Hampshire
Born:	June 29, 1959	in: Melrose, MA
M Married:	December 28, 1988	in: North Reading, MA
Spouse:	Virginia Smith	

50th anniversary celebration

My brother, Robert was killed in Korea in 1951. I remember very little about him. The only thing remember about Robert is that when he walked through the door, he had to duck. He brought me a teddy bear from over there. I don't have it; I don't know what happened to it. He did his tour of duty and came home, but while he was there he had married a Japanese woman, and so he "re-upped" for the sole purpose of getting together with his wife.

I think that Dottie Jeanes and Rev. Sweet from our church tried to make some connection so that they could meet up together when Robert re-enlisted. He understood that when the boat got to Japan, he was going to be able to get off, but when they got there, they said that no one could get off, so Robert was not able to see his wife again. He went on to Korea. He was driving a truck, and the truck got blown up, and that's how he died. So Robert was never able to see the woman that he married again.

I only have a picture of her. Jean talked to her after Robert passed away and said, "You're welcome to come here, because you're part of our family." But she felt like she would be more comfortable living in Japan with her folks.

I was able to see the letter that my Mom wrote about Robert's death, and through that letter and the one she wrote my grandmother when Herbert died, I saw her compassion and her love for her children. When she was writing to Gram about Robert, she said that when they buried Robert, they handed her the flag, and she said they "… can keep it for all I care, they took my son." Then she said that Donald could have it when he got old enough. That gave me a sense of how much my mother loved her children.

When I grew up and realized what Robert did for our country, I made a promise that I would visit his grave every Memorial Day, but it did not happen, because I moved away. In 2005, when I moved back to Massachusetts, I found out that they have a ceremony first thing every Memorial Day at seven o'clock in the morning. The honor guard and the militia men march into the cemetery, and they call the roll of all the veterans buried in the cemeteries in town. The Riverside Cemetery is where my brother Robert is buried. They also include my brother Elwood in the roll beginning in 2010 as that was the year he passed away.

day. Robert was put in the tomb until spring. A full military funeral was given him. I am pleased to think and know what is left of his body is home here. The Legion enlarged a snap of Robert and framed it and gave it to me. It is wonderful. They gave me a 9' x 5' flag. The gov. can have it for all I care. I don't think much of it in exchange for the life of my boy. I had Billy put it up in the trunk. If Ronald wants it later O.K. but it will stay.

Mom's letter to Gram about Robert's funeral

Robert and his wife, Chico

Robert's best friend - each year he puts a geranium on his grave – and carries a picture of him still in his wallet.

The first time I attended the ceremony, I was very impressed, and I asked Gordon Hall, one of the militia men, if he would take a picture of me by my brother's grave. He did that, and he told me that he had known my mother. She was Sunday School superintendent when he attended the First Baptist Church of North Reading. He said she was one of the nicest persons he ever met. That was nice to hear. Then another man behind me asked, "Are you Robert's sister?" When I said yes, he said, "I was his best friend. My name is Lyman Fancy. We used to hang out together—used to race cars. Every year since 1953, I've put a geranium on his stone." I was very, very impressed that he still had a picture of my brother in his wallet. He was obviously very special to Robert.

Honoring my brother, Robert, at the cemetery each Memorial Day
where they call the roll. Now that my brother, Elwood Jr, has passed
away his name is called, as well.

The next in line is William who we call Billy. He married Judy Marshall and had 6 children. He was deacon at the First Baptist Church in North Reading for many years. An interesting fact about Billy is that Gram allowed him to be called Billy even though everyone else had to use their proper names – no nicknames around her. He served in the Air Force. He worked as a mechanic and could fi x anything that had an engine to it. He was an aircraft mechanic. He was the crew chief for the B47. It was a 6 engine jet, weighing 97 tons and held 105,000 lbs. of fuel. It was used to carry bombs. The Red Cross arranged for Billy to come home as mom was dying. He felt like she waited to see him. She died the night after he came home.

Billy's wife left him with the 6 children and was devastated. He later married Janet who had 6 children also and ended up with quite a houseful. I think the only way he made it through all that is trusting in God for whatever they needed. A strong faith in God can carry you through whatever you have to go through. Billy became very active upon retirement. He and Janet moved to Vermont where he helped build a Pregnancy Crisis Center to help young girls decide to have their babies instead of having an abortion. He also completed "mud outs" and prepared the removal of trees that had been affected by disasters in many locations as they rebuilt houses for those victims of the disaster.

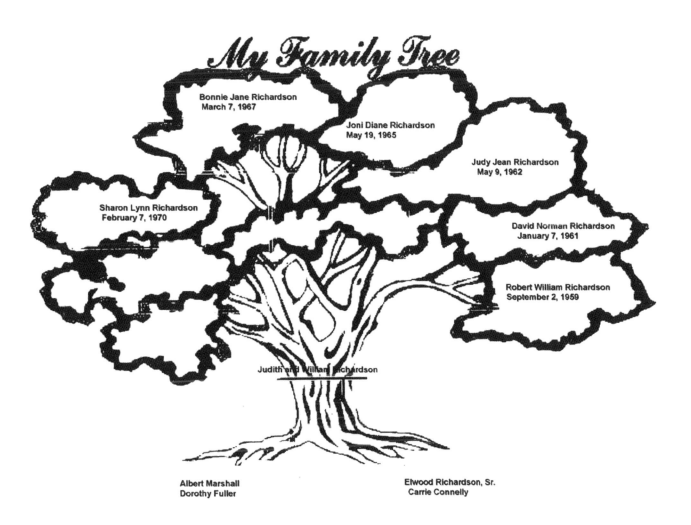

My Family Tree

Bonnie Jane Richardson
March 7, 1967

Joni Diane Richardson
May 19, 1965

Judy Jean Richardson
May 9, 1962

Sharon Lynn Richardson
February 7, 1970

David Norman Richardson
January 7, 1961

Robert William Richardson
September 2, 1959

Judith and William Richardson

Albert Marshall
Dorothy Fuller

Elwood Richardson, Sr.
Carrie Connelly

Husband: William Arthur Richardson

Born: March 13, 1934   in: Somerville, MA

Married: June 2, 1958   in: North Reading, MA

Father: Elwood Lyndon Richardson, Sr.

Mother: Carrie Mable Connelly

Other Spouses: Janet Pettingill

Wife: Judith Dearborn Marshall

Born: October 7, 1937   in: Woburn, MA

Father: Albert L. Marshall

Mother: Dorothy Fuller

CHILDREN:

1. Name: Robert William Richardson

   Born: September 2, 1959   in: Melrose, MA

M Married: January 26, 1980   in: Andover, MA

   Spouse: Kim Michelle Smith

   Other spouses: Barbara Fitch

2. Name: David Norman Richardson

   Born: January 7, 1961   in: Woburn, MA

M Married:

   Spouse:

3. Name: Judy Jean Richardson

   Born: May 9, 1962   in: Woburn, MA

F Married: January 31, 1985   in: Dallas, Texas

   Spouse: Ahmad Abumlhem

4. Name: Joni Diane Richardson

   Born: May 19,1965   in: Woburn, MA

F Married: May 1998   in: North Reading, MA

   Spouse: Robert Conroy

   Other spouses: Howard Foh

5. Name: Bonnie Jane Richardson

   Born: March 7, 1967 in: Woburn, MA

F Married: June 9, 2001 In Mt. Barre, MA

   Spouse: Lance R. Abare

   Other spouses: Patrick Welch

6. Name: Sharon Lynn Richardson

   Born: February 7, 1970   in: Woburn, MA

F Married: August 25, 1990   in: North Reading, MA

   Spouse: Corey Rand

The next in line is Charlie. Charlie named his oldest son Charlie, and then that son Charlie named his son Charlie III, so the name has been passed down in the family. Charlie was married to Ruthie, a girl I went to school with. He was a really handsome guy. To me, he looked like Elvis Presley. When my classmate told me she was dating Charlie, and they were gonna get married, I flippantly said, "Well, I'll always have him. He's my brother." I wish I had not said that.

At one point in his life, he got in with the wrong crowd and had to spend time in jail. The family was always supportive of him and he regained his acceptance into society. Charlie was a perfectionist. He worked in construction and was put in charge of a crew that was responsible in erecting the cloverleaf on 128/129 and Route 1 which allowed access to Wakefield, Reading, Saugus and Peabody, Massachusetts. Billy remembers how much of a perfectionist he was. He remembers him excited that he found a perfect way to clear the ice off the windshield of the car. He used sandpaper and got a clear view except when the sun shone on it and saw that he had scratched it all and it had to be replaced.

Charlie had six children. When his youngest and only daughter, Justine was very young, he was hit by a drunk driver. He was standing by the road helping someone else fix their motorcycle—he rode motorcycles—and a drunk driver swerved and pulled him down the road. He was brought to the hospital. They called me to see if I could come because I had the same blood as he had and could do a direct transfusion. I said "of course" and made arrangement to make the trip. Bobby and I didn't have the money but Jr. wired us $200 so we could make the trip. At first he seemed to be doing well, but then they said, "Well, we're going to have to amputate a leg to save his life." They did that, but in another couple of days he had passed away before I arrived.

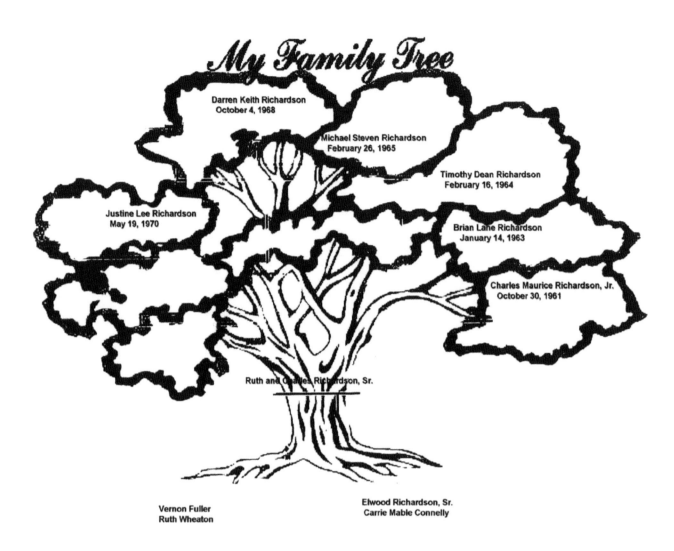

My Family Tree

Darren Keith Richardson
October 4, 1968

Michael Steven Richardson
February 26, 1965

Timothy Dean Richardson
February 16, 1964

Justine Lee Richardson
May 19, 1970

Brian Lane Richardson
January 14, 1963

Charles Maurice Richardson, Jr.
October 30, 1961

Ruth and Charles Richardson, Sr.

Vernon Fuller
Ruth Wheaton

Elwood Richardson, Sr.
Carrie Mable Connelly

Husband: Charles Maurice Richardson, Sr.

Born:	December 8, 1935	in: Somerville, MA
Married:	April 8, 1961	in: North Reading, MA
Died:	September 8, 1973	in: Concord, NH
Father:	Elwood Lyndon Richardson, Sr.	
Mother:	Carrie Mable Connelly	

Wife: Ruth Ann Fuller

Born:	April 23, 1943	in: Melrose, MA
Father:	Vernon Fuller	
Mother:	Ruth Wheaton	

Other Spouse: George Leslie Hodgkins, Jr.

CHILDREN:

1. Name: Charles Maurice Richardson, Jr

    Born: October 30, 1961   in: Melrose, MA

M   Married: November 7, 1987   in: Stonington, Ct.

    Spouse: Pamela Jeanne Donovan

2. Name: Brian Lane Richardson

    Born: January 14, 1963   in: Melrose, MA

M   Married: April 3, 1999   in: Niagara Falls, NY

    Spouse: Cindi McNulty

3. Name: Timothy Dean Richardson

    Born: February 16, 1964   in: Melrose, MA

M   Married: July 25, 1998   in: Norwich, Ct.

    Spouse: Ruth Clark

    Other spouse: Kim Whitlock

4. Name: Michael Steven Richardson

    Born: February 26,1965   in: Melrose, MA

M   Married: April 20, 1987   in: East Grenich, RI

    Spouse: Missy Burnell

5. Name: Darren Keith Richardson

    Born: October 4, 1968   in: Melrose, MA

M   Married: April 15, 2000   in: Versailles, Ct.

    Spouse: Sarah Jane Black

6. Name: Justine Lee Richardson

    Born: May 19, 1970   in: Melrose, MA F

    Married: December 5, 1998   in: Everett, MA

    Spouse: Steve Bennett

At that time, I was living in Oklahoma, and my husband, who drove the whole way, and I and the three small children in a Volkswagen traveled to Massachusetts for the funeral. When we got there, we were told that the family could see the body if they wanted to, but they didn't suggest that I do that. I agreed with them, but I think that was a wrong decision on my part.

When I got back home, I began having nightmares of my brother, Charlie, lying in a casket, and his leg moved. I really had a tough time dealing with it, because I didn't look. Because of that, in preparing my funeral and services, I've asked that the children at least have the option to see my body. I don't want them to have nightmares because they didn't have a chance to see my body.

Charlie and Ruthie

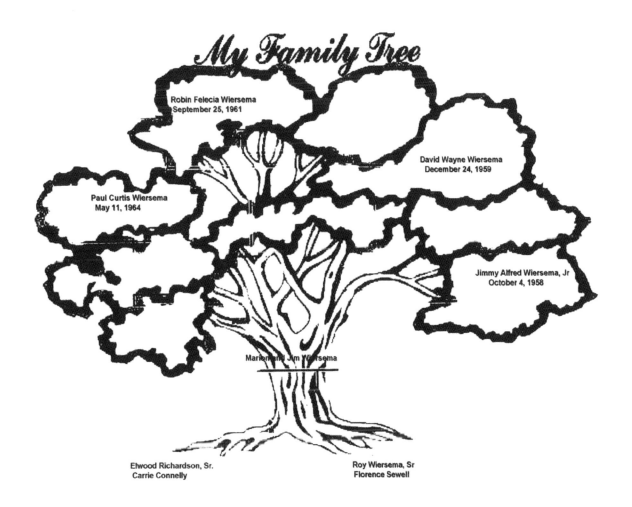

My Family Tree

Robin Felecia Wiersema
September 25, 1961

David Wayne Wiersema
December 24, 1959

Paul Curtis Wiersema
May 11, 1964

Jimmy Alfred Wiersema, Jr
October 4, 1958

Marion and Jim Wiersema

Elwood Richardson, Sr.
Carrie Connelly

Roy Wiersema, Sr
Florence Sewell

Marion is next in line. She was my only sister. Because my stepmother didn't like me and told me I was retarded, she wouldn't teach me how to do anything in the kitchen, because I made a mess. Along with Jean, my sister explained things about nylons and shaving legs and being modest and stuff like that.

Husband: Jimmy Alfred Wiersema, Sr.

Born:	February 28, 1938	in: Fort Sill, OK
Married:	March 25, 1958	in: Otis A.F.B. Barnstable, MA
Died:	May 19, 2007	in: Wisconsin
Father:	Roy Wiersema, Sr.	
Mother:	Florence Ellen Sewell	
Other Spouses:	June	

Wife:	Marion Louise Richardson		

Born:	November 2, 1938	in: Boston, MA
Died:	August 2, 2004	in: Appleton, WI
Father:	Elwood Lyndon Richardson, Sr.	
Mother:	Carrie Mable Connelly	

CHILDREN:

1.	Name:	Jimmy Alfred Wiersema, Jr.	
	Born:	October 4, 1958	in: Wareham, MA
M	Married:	October 7, 1977	in: Apache, OK
	Spouse:	Pamela Renee White	

2.	Name:	David Wayne Wiersema	
	Born:	December 24, 1959	in: Melrose, MA
M	Married:	September 26, 1987	in: Lewisville, TX
	Spouse:	Carolyn Sue Mayo	

3.	Name:	Robin Felecia Wiersema	
M	Born:	September 25, 1961	in: Lawton, OK
	Married:	November 5, 1983	in: Highland Village, OK
	Spouse:	Keith Allen Mack	

4.	Name:	Paul Curtis Wiersema	
	Born:	May 11, 1964	in: Lawton, OK
M	Married:	August 16, 1986	in: Lewisville, TX
	Spouse:	Kathy Lina Dunnam	

My sister and her husband were missionaries in Brazil for several years. This article was in the winter 2002 issue of North American Mission Board, A publication for Southern Baptist Adult Mission Volunteers in North America.

Reflecting the Heart of the MSC

Soft-spoken MSC Missionaries of the Year, Jim and Marion Wiersema, say "yes" to God, even before He fills in the details.

They say yes before God fills in the details. That, among other qualities, notes Mike Riggins, Missionary Mobilization Associate, NAMB sets apart Jim and Marion Wiersema, Mission Service Corps missionaries of the Year of 2001. From a field of 2, 600 MSC missionaries, the Wiersemas were selected.

"Jim and Marion reflect the heart of Mission Service Corps," notes Riggins. "We mobilize people who say yes to God's call, and go wherever He leads, extending our borders to touch others' greatest needs. In 1003, when I met the Wiersemas, I was impressed by the clarity of their call. Nothing else really mattered."

The Wiersemas had been involved in an Experiencing God Bible study, which instructs believers to find where God is at work and to join Him.

About the same time, Wiersema lost his job – and a call came from Oshkosh, Wisconsin, asking the Wiersemas to help start a church there.

With a desire to experience what God might have for their lives, in June the Wiersemas met with Baptists in Oshkosh. "On the way back home we decided that was where God wanted us to go," Wiersema says. "I decided I can be unemployed in Wisconsin as easy as I can be unemployed in Texas."

God confirmed that call with a tax refund to pay off all their bills except for the house

During that visit to Wisconsin, the Wiersemas had explored the possibility of working through the MSSC. When they got back to Texas, they contacted MSC coordinators Sam and Polly Pearis who arranged for them to attend

MSC orientation. "There was a waiting list to attend, but enough dropped out for us to be able to go."

Later, when Wiersema stopped by his church to pick up MSC forms, he received an envelope addressed, "To Jim and Marion Wiersema from Someone Who Cares." "When we opened the envelope there were 11 one-hundred dollar bills inside to help with moving expenses."

Once in Wisconsin, the Wiersemas began working on a church start that had failed on three other occasions. They began a Bible study, and worked with the five adults who were holding the mission together. As the mission grew, they prepared to call a pastor. In 1999, the mission became Celebration Fellowship Baptist Church.

Wiersema's next challenge was to serve as interim pastor at Bethany Baptist Church. "The first Sunday," says Wiersema, "eight attended." Wiersema opened their eyes to the field all around them. Today, Bethany averages 50 in attendance and has started three missions. Notes a member: Our church is deeply moved by this couple's true servant heart."

Now the Wiersemas are church strengtheners for the 21- county Bay Lakes Association. They moved to Appleton where they encourage churches and find ways to serve them. Wiersema is also interim pastor at Fellowship Baptist Church in Waupaaca. "Very few lay people get to fill a pulpit. The Lord keeps opening doors and as we walk through them the Lord continues to pour out blessings."

Sinde the Wiersemas moved to Wisconsin, they have taken two mission trips to Brazil, and one to Siberia to help plant a church. "On one trip to Brazil we saw 4,000 people accept Christ in two weeks," Wiersema says. "The team was made up of volunteers, everyday lay people working with missionaries."

This year, Wiersema was elected moderator of the association. Dennis Hansen, director of missions, says that's usually a role for pastors. Says Hansen: "Jim and Marion are willing to do everything to help out the churches. I don't recall them ever saying no."

What is MSC Missionary of the Year?

Criteria for this distinction includes commitment to and effectiveness in evangelism, church planting or ministry; outstanding performance in achieving assigned asks; tenure; unusual commitment to our Lord's service; positive representation of Mission Service Corps, and being on "on-mission Christian."

Jim and Marion Wiersema were taken back by the honor. Says Jim, "We've just listened to the Lord."

Prayer request: Pray for the people in this part of the country. Many were baptized as infants and don't see the need for further commitment. Pray that God will give us wisdom and stamina.

Marion and Jim

God really used them. Uncle Jim was just about to retire when his company let him go. He decided that it was time to go into missionary work, and God provided for them to do that. They turned a situation that was really ugly into one that honored God, and that was very cool in my estimation.

I got a call after one of their trips Marion had gone in for exploratory surgery, and there was cancer in her pancreas. It was the very, very beginnings of it, and they had very high hopes of eradicating it. She started on chemo and radiation. After that bout, she was given a clean bill of health. They were living in Wisconsin at the time, and I spent Thanksgiving week of 2003 with them. It was my birthday, and we celebrated her cure from cancer as well. We went to Wal-Mart and had our pictures made. Our brothers were delighted to receive pictures of their only sisters.

Marion and I

I went home to Texas. But the first part of July in 2004, I got a call from Uncle Jim that the cancer was back and with a vengeance. Marion was on chemo again and within a week, Uncle Jim called to say that the doctor had said the chemo wasn't doing any good. They were going to take her off chemo and just have her home in hospice care.

I called my brothers – Donald, Junior and Billy – and told them, and we all, except for Junior – went out there. Junior wasn't able to go because of his health. He needed a hip replacement, but they wouldn't do it because he was in his eighties. He would not be able to make the trip even in an airplane. So Billy and Janet came from Vermont, Donald and Maria came from New Hampshire and I from Texas. She talked to Lisa on the phone and Junior and asked about my children and where Tommy was living. Bubba called to talk to her but she thought it was Scotty. She was always concerned about others.

During our visit we had one very special afternoon. We surrounded Marion's bed, and we asked her things about our mom, and if she knew mom's favorite verse, she said it was "Believe in the Lord, Jesus Christ and you will be saved and your household." I know mom had prayed for all of us. Marion's favorite song was "What a Friend We Have in Jesus." We had a very awesome time just visiting, and there weren't any tears at the time. God gave us peace.

Billy and Marion used to squabble quite a bit growing up. I wasn't there, but I heard about it. When Billy came into Marion's room on that visit – he's very outspoken – he said, I heard you said I never come to visit you." And to that, Marion replied, "Well, you're here now." It just set the tone for a very special afternoon.

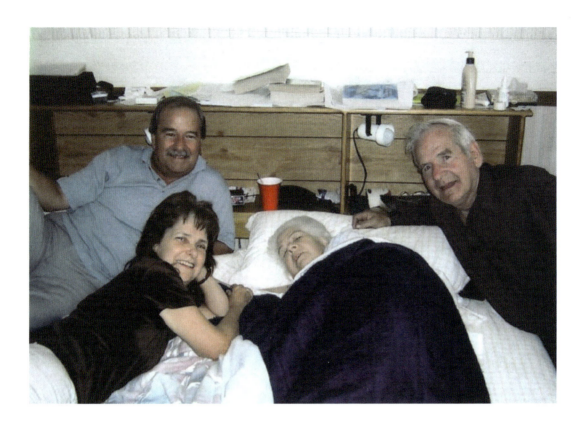

My sister dying of pancreatic cancer and we all are spending time with her

Donald and Billy left and I stayed another day. Her oldest son, Jimmy, Jr. who I call Buster had arrived and as I left I went in to give her a kiss and tell her I loved her. She said I love you, too. I also asked her if she saw mom before I did to tell her we all (all her children) were coming. She said she would do that.

Toward the end of July, I made a trip to Massachusetts and brought the picture that I had taken of Junior talking to Marion on the phone. He was so thrilled to get that since he was not able to go.

On August 2, 2004, Uncle Jim called to say she had died. We (my brothers and I) chose not to go to the funeral. We had already said our goodbyes.

Scotty and his family, however, went to the funeral.

A couple of years after that, Uncle Jim remarried. He died in his sleep two years later, so they are both deceased now. I had a great support team in Texas; I was in a "cell" group with Suzie and Tim Brown. I talked to Suzie and she said I should have a good cry. That was very therapeutic. I did and I also talked to my best friend, Alisa. She was right there for me. We spent the day together. She told me to find a picture of Marion and bring it with me and we were going out to eat lunch and she told me to be prepared to cry in public.

This was new for me but I trusted Alisa. We went to lunch and then in the shopping mall we stopped at a "Build a Bear" where I was to make a bear to remember my sister. I chose a Koala bear because she had gone to Brazil on mission trips. I chose an Angel shirt because Marion and Jim's song was "You are my special Angel", and ribbons for the hair. We took the small photo and stuffed it inside the bear and chose the sound of "I love you" to be included when it was pressed. It was a most special time of grief shared with a friend.

Donald and I were the only children who lived with my step-mother and father. The others were old enough to be on their own or lived with Jr.

Donald is two years older than I am. We went to the same high school. I remember he was very, very smart. Donald skipped school once in a while, and his teachers would say to me, "He doesn't even have to open a book; he just has to show up for school." And then he wouldn't show up for school.

I was very concerned for him. He was a senior, and I was an underclassman, so we didn't hang around that much together, but I wanted him to graduate. He had a car at that time—I rode the school bus– but if it snowed, and he couldn't get the car out, I would get up early and shovel the driveway out so that he would go to school.

His teachers would tell me, "Just encourage him to come to school; that's all he has to do is show up. He doesn't even have to crack a book." He was really very smart, and later on in years when I told him, "I know you've always been smart," he said, "No, I just remember things." It wasn't a show-off y thing for him. He's just smart, but he doesn't say anybody else isn't smart.

Donald once told me that he was a little bit of a problem for my mom behavior-wise. One afternoon when he was to spend the afternoon up in his room, he crawled out the window and went out to play with friends. They were ice skating, and he mistook some foam for ice and went under the ice. One of his brothers—or one of the friends— pulled him up. He was obviously soaking wet, and it was a terrible scare, because if they hadn't seen him go under, he would not have been saved.

He walked into the house expecting the worst from mom, because he was supposed to be up in his room, and here he was, soaking wet. He went to the door, and she got him all dried and everything. She sat him on her lap, and he remembers her saying, "You need to give your heart to Jesus." He said, "And I did." That point was the beginning of his journey. It's always a process, but he said, "I can look back now and see that that was the beginning of my faith journey. For my mother to do that—she didn't whoop me, she just told me that I needed to give my heart to Jesus." Again my mom showing the love she had for her children.

Donald and I continued to live with my stepmother after my father died. The others were old enough that they were kind of on their own. Whoever needed a house lived with Junior, my older brother.

Donald joined the army as soon as he graduated from high school. I didn't hear from him for a while, because when I graduated, I left New England and went to live with my sister. He wasn't too crazy about the army. He repaired trucks and tanks. He served in Saran, France until he got out. He did his time and then he got out.

He was in the Vietnam War, and of course the effect that had on everybody— everybody thought it was a useless war. It was very discouraging for them when they came back. I'm encouraged to hear now that people have reneged on that and say that all of our serviceman made an impact on our freedom, including those who went to Vietnam. He went in Nov '61, went to Fort Dix NJ for basic training, went to Aberdeen MD for training on repair of trucks and tanks, He went to Saran, France until they let him out Oct '64. In France he was repairing vehicles to keep the troops moving. Later he was in charge of the motor pool and the headquarters barracks where he made SP5 rank.

My Family Tree

Lisa Marie Richardson
September 10, 1977

Joseph Anthony Richardson
June 5, 1975

Derek Michael Richardson
October 10, 1969

Maria and Donald Richardson

Mary Tascano
Joseph Pellegrino

Elwood Richardson, Sr
Carrie Connelly

Husband: Donald John Richardson

Born: April 21, 1943   in: Winchester, MA
Married: May 7, 1967   in: Reading, MA
Father: Elwood Lyndon Richardson, Sr.
Mother: Carrie Mable Connelly

Wife: Maria Theresa Pellegrino

Born: July 24, 1943   in: Boston, MA

Father: Joseph E. Pellegrino

Mother: Mary Tascano

CHILDREN:

---

1. Name: Derek Michael Richardson

	Born:	October 10, 1969	in: Lynfield, MA
M	Married:	June 30, 2002	
	Spouse:	Renee Sue Lussier	

2.	Name:	Joseph Anthony Richardson	
	Born:	June 5, 1975	in: Lynfield, MA
M	Married:		
	Spouse:		

3.	Name:	Lisa Marie Richardson	
	Born:	September 10, 1977	in: Atkinson, NH
F	Died:	November 19, 2006	in: Atkinson, NH

Picture of my mother that Aunt Evelyn gave me while at the gas station with Bobby

Mr. and Mrs. Anderson were a couple in the church—no relation to us. They had three boys, and they always wanted a girl, and when they learned that my mother could not take care of me, they told my mother that they would watch me every time she needed help. I have actually thought that I stayed with them the whole time, but my brother Donald tells me that I came back home on occasion, when my mother felt good enough to care for me.

The Andersons were very, very special. Mrs. Anderson raised cocker spaniels, and I was allowed to pick out one puppy that I could keep. I picked out a black and white cocker spaniel. It had white on its paws, so I called it Snowshoes. It was my dog, and it was kept at the Andersons', even if I went back to my mother's. I don't honestly remember going back to my mother's, but Donald says that I did. Mrs. Anderson was a schoolteacher, and she helped me in school. Her being a teacher helped me feel comfortable in school. She was my teacher in third grade. I didn't realize that she was until talking to my friend, Trudy Jeanes and talking about a teacher in school that liked me and she pointed out that she was Mrs. Anderson.

Pop Anderson—I called him Pop—was very, very special too. He and I spent a lot of time together. We were very active in the First Baptist Church in North Reading. We were painting a new wing of the church, the Robertson Wing, named after the pastor at the time, Rev. Earton Roberton, and there I was standing with a bucket of paint with all the other guys. There were very few girls or women, but we helped paint the Robertson Wing. I remember Pop saying that I always came back (each time my mother would need help in caring for me), just like a bad penny. He was really always pleased when I came back.

I kept in touch with Pop up until a few years before he died in 2002. He remarried several times after Mrs. Pauline Anderson passed away, but each of those wives passed away too. Pop tried to stay in his house, but he could never get warm enough, and so he was in a nursing home in Maine. I visited him whenever I came to New England, and he was always real pleased to see me.

The last time I saw him was in the nursing home, and he just said he was getting tired and trying to keep warm. He died at 94 years old. They were a very special couple. I was very impressed that they were just another couple at the church who saw a need and filled it for my mom.

Where Pop and I among other members of First Baptist were painting the church wing

First Baptist Church of North Reading

Pop (Mr. Anderson) and me - who I lived
with while my mother was sick in my
younger days

My father married Eva Flibbotte August 3, 1953 very soon after my mother died on April 18, 1953.

After my father remarried Eva, whenever there was no school she said I had to go to work with my dad, because she didn't want me around the house. I used to go and play by the train tracks and play on the rocks or in the car, and we would have lunch together. I don't remember too much of the conversations. I remember playing in the rocks. I don't know what I did, but I occupied myself until he came for lunch, and then we talked and ate. Later in my life, for some reason, I found consolation in walking the railroad tracks when I was extremely hurt by my second husband, James Bouland.

I remember one day when we didn't have school, my friend Susan Place invited me to go swimming in her pool that day. My stepmother said, "No, you're going to work with your dad." When I got into the car, I was crying, and Daddy asked me how come I was crying. "Well," I said, "Susan asked me to go swimming, and I wanted to go swimming." His comment was, "Don't you want to spend time with me?" I'm extremely glad I have that memory of him.

I was ten years old when I learned that my father had drowned. We lived in a small town, North Reading, Massachusetts and my friend and I had been walking downtown. We were coming back, and the little girl next door poked her head out the door and said, "Your father drowned in Maine." Her mother pulled her in by the hair of the head, and so me and my girlfriend, Susan Place, sat on my front stairs, because I didn't want to go in and talk to my stepmother.

I asked Susan if she thought that that was true, and we sat there for a few minutes. Then, we saw the father take the little girl who'd said that out. We knew it was just the mother there, so we walked over there, and we asked her if that was true, and she asked us to come in. She asked me if I wanted a cookie. I remember I was very angry, because she was saying, "Yes, that's true," but she asked me if I wanted a cookie. I don't remember anything about the conversation, just that she asked and that it made me angry.

I don't remember what happened when I finally went into the house and talked to my stepmother, either. I don't think she told me much. I was told I could not go to the funeral. I don't know why that was.

My father had gone to Maine to make all the arrangements for when my grandfather passed away. Grampa John was living with us at the time, and he was getting on in years. So my father was in Maine to make the arrangements, and he went fishing in a secluded pond, in a canoe. He went with another fellow. We don't know many details, but we were told the other guy hurt his shoulder and couldn't help my dad. Evidently, the canoe capsized.

My grandmother refused to let them do an autopsy, so I don't know … I know that my father could swim very well. In fact, I believe he taught me how to swim.

He's buried in Maine with my mom in the Sandy Hill Cemetery in Palermo, Maine. In fact, that's where I'm going to be buried. There's several lots there that my grandmother had paid for, and they're not used, and I have mine all arranged. When I first came to home in 2005, I stayed with my brother, Jr. and he said Gram had bought him a plot in Maine but he didn't want it because he wanted to be buried next to his wife, Jean in the Riverside Cemetery in North Reading. I asked if I could have it and he said yes, so I wrote to the director of the Sandy Hill Cemetery in Palermo, Maine and he said there are actually 24 plots that she bought. Two of them are where my mom and dad are buried so there are 22 plots left. They cannot sell them to anyone. They belong to us. So I supplied the rest of the family with that information but most won't to use that cemetery because it is so far away from where they live. I however, want to be buried there. The Croswell funeral home knows exactly where they're to bury me—next to my mom and dad. I am in the process of setting a set of "fawns" on the site. I have also contacted the director of that cemetery to say the family will be glad to have anyone who needs a plot to use them, just call and let us know.

I had a lot of negative things in high school, because there were cliques. I had wanted to be a cheerleader, but they said I wasn't pretty enough. I had a couple of teachers—Miss Catalina and Mr. Lazemby—who helped me with self-esteem, so that I could make it through.

Trudy Jeanes was one classmate who became a friend. Her mother, Ruth, was a secretary at the high school. She used to let me work in the office, and that was a help to me. It made me feel important—I wasn't rich enough to be with rich kids, and I couldn't hang out with kids aft er school, because I was expected to come right home. But some teachers, Trudy, and her mom, and the church were a big help. It was really a help to have a couple of teachers who were encouraging … along with Mrs. Anderson.

I remember Trudy Jeanes's Aunt Dottie from the First Baptist Church of North

Dottie Jeanes - our missionary in Japan for 35 years

Reading. She was a missionary to Japan for thirty-five years. She wrote a book called *Accepting the Challenge* when she returned. It is available at the Park Street Church in Boston and also at Trinity Evangelical Church in North Reading, Massachusetts. When she came back from her service and I had moved back from Texas, she needed help with her laundry and cleaning her house weekly. Nothing really strenuous or anything, but I was a little perturbed with the church that they didn't provide that for her. I thought we needed to support her, since she was our missionary from our church for that long a time. Maybe that's what I was there for. I worked and helped her each week get her laundry. She couldn't carry them downstairs. She could drive and cook her meals and stuff like that, but some of the stuff she needed help with, and that's what I did—and I didn't let her pay me of course.

During that time, Trudy asked Dottie and me to come to her home in Twin Mountain, New Hampshire where she lived with her husband. She had a separate cottage for guests. We went there a couple of times and spent a couple of weekends there before Trudy became sick. We shared stories about our children and how we prayed for them all the time.

I found out that Trudy had a brain tumor, and she came to Dottie's house and stayed for a while. She had one surgery, and they checked the growth, and it had grown again. She had another surgery, and they checked it, and it was still growing. She finally said, "I can't go through another set of chemo." And she said that "that's all," and so she passed away shortly after that.

Another high school friend was named Kathleen Orben. We used to hang around a lot together. In school, they used to say that we were probably joined at the hip. She was an underclassman, but we were very close. We did a lot of "girly chit-chat," and I was able to share what was frustrating with my stepmother.

I think my stepmother knew Kathleen was my friend, but I don't think I was ever allowed to bring her over to the house. I was allowed to go over there. I didn't really like to bring my friends over to my house. When Kathleen and I were together, we were either at school, or over at her house, or at the church. Kathleen wasn't as regular at church as Trudy was, but we used to spend time there too, on extra activities and stuff.

Kathleen's mother was very understanding—she had known my mother and understood the difficulty I had with my step-mother. They weren't family, but it was a small community where friends were like family. We did as much as we could together, but only during the school hours and, I guess, when we had free time in the school.

Kathleen came to visit me when I was pregnant with my third child. We sent Christmas cards, but we didn't keep in touch much more than that. At one point when I came back to visit New England, I left a note at her house. She came to visit me at my brother, Jr's home where I was visiting and told me that she had cancer, but that she was doing well and just struggling along. She looked very thin, and I was glad to see her, but there was no real follow-up. That was the last time I saw her. I was hoping to see her the next time I came back to Massachusetts for a visit, but then I found out that she had passed away. I don't know where she was buried, and I don't know the circumstances. I'm sure it was the cancer.

My math teacher, Mr. Lazemby, was another one who encouraged me. He gave me an A, and I was not sure why, because I always struggled with math. I kinda thought he made a mistake, but I was afraid to say anything. I can't tell you how I finally approached him, but when I did he said, "No, you earned it. I didn't give that to you. You did a very good job this semester, and your understanding of what we covered and you can do it." My grandmother helped me some with math, but actually hearing it from a teacher was a help too.

When I was in high school, I used to get in trouble for sneaking out to see my future husband. I met Bobby at the gas station next to where my brother lived in Reading, Massachusetts. At fi rst, I didn't think he was very handsome, but it just kinda grew on me.

The library and the police station were between my house and the school. One time, Bobby met me after school, and we went to the library and hung out a little bit. Well, my stepmother called the police and said that I wasn't home when I was supposed to be. About that time, we walked into the police station to visit them, and a policeman said, "Your mother's on the phone." He said they had to bring me home in their police car.

My stepmother thought I would learn my lesson, because the police had to bring me home, but I thought that was kinda cool. I'd visited the police before, and I considered them my friends.

Shortly after that, my stepmother called my brother and said that she couldn't handle me. I'm not sure if it was the incident just above or the hayride that caused that phone call. Bobby went with me on a hayride with the church. There was a wagon for the younger kids and one for the older kids. We got on the wrong wagon with the little kids, and we were making out. We'd ask the kids, "Can you time us and see how long we can kiss?" Well, it got back to the pastor, and he called my stepmother.

I think a combination of the two—getting caught at the library and the hayride—was why she called my brother and said, "I can't handle her." My oldest brother, Jr. said, "Well, you come live with us." I didn't have a problem with that, 'cause I liked going over there. They had seven kids, and I had someone to play with.

I asked, "Do I have to break up with Bobby?" And they said, "No." But when I got over there, they said I had to break up with Bobby. I was not happy with that, but their third child, Helen—my niece—and I were very, very close. I'd write letters to Bobby, and Helen would take them over to the gas station. Then Bobby would write me a letter back, and Helen would bring it to me, so Bobby and I conversed back and forth like that. That came to an end when I had to go back to the school. If I had stayed at my brother's, I would have had to go to a different school, so they sent me back to my stepmother. Helen and I spent a lot of time together. She evidently saw me shaving my legs in the bathtub and decided she wanted to do that, too so she did but ran the razor straight up the middle of her leg on the bone and was bleeding all over the place. That was the only time I saw Jean upset with me. She did correct me in a most loving way.

Bobby used to call on the phone, and the phone was in my stepmother's bedroom, so she was always the one to answer. He'd call and tell her that she should let me go to extracurricular activities—that it was good for me, and so, when he called, she would say, "It's the voice of experience calling." When she said that, I knew it was Bobby on the phone.

At one point, I said that I wanted to meet Bobby's mother. They lived in Boston, and we were gonna take the train into Boston. For some reason, my stepmother said that that was okay, and so we went to meet Bobby's mother. He had planned it so that we took the last train in.

I met his mother and his stepfather, and we got along just fi ne. But then I told them we needed to get back, and Bobby said, "We need to get back." We ran all the way to the train station, and sure enough, the last train had gone. Later on, I found out Bobby planned it that way.

I called my stepmother and told her that we didn't catch the last train, so we were gonna have to spend the night in Boston. She didn't have any idea what was going on, and she just automatically said "yes." I thought that was very unusual, but then she started hollering at me because of the hayride.

It didn't make a whole lot of sense to me at the time, I could be sleeping with this guy but she was worried about what I did at a church hayride. We spent the night, but of course Bobby's mother and stepfather were there. We came back the next morning.

Bobby eventually told me, "I wanted you to spend the night." He was a little promiscuous himself, but not with me.

I used to walk over to the gas station where Bobby worked. It was seven miles from my house on 127 Elm Street in North Reading, Massachusetts. My aunt Evelyn came to visit one Saturday morning. Bobby and I were sitting in the back of the gas station and we were making out, and in walked my aunt Evelyn.

She had a picture of my mother, who had died, and she said, "Here, I want you to have this." I think it was an attempt to break us up, because Bobby was Catholic and I was Baptist and did not approve and was trying to say if my mother was alive she would not approve either. They also thought that I was not being responsible, and so they were trying to separate us.

I tried to explain to them that from the beginning of the relationship, I told Bobby that we weren't going to do anything sexually. I wanted to be married in a white dress, and that's how it was. But they didn't believe me. I guess Bobby might have had a reputation.

LILLIAN R. RICHARDSON
127 Elm Street
"Lil"

Ambition: Secretary
Favorite Memory: Summer of 1961 in Maine
Pet Peeve: No car
Favorite Pastime: Talking on the phone
Activities: NOREHISC; Prom Committees

The thing that goes the farthest towards making life worthwhile is just a pleasant smile.

44

A page from my high school yearbook

When I graduated from high school, my stepmother didn't want me to stay with her, so I went and lived with Marion in Oklahoma. She told me I had a choice – Gram or Marion – I knew it was not really a choice, she would decide the opposite of what I wanted so I told her Gram and sure enough she decided I would go to live with Marion. She had three kids ages, 5, 4 and 2 years old, and when I was there she had her fourth. Two weeks after the baby, Paul, was born, Marion had to go back in the hospital and have gall stones and a diseased gall bladder taken out, so at seventeen years old, I was taking care of a newborn baby and three other kids. That was quite a chore for me. I did love them dearly. Robin, the youngest, and I shared a room and would play a game each night when we were told to go to bed. I would say "Goodnight, Sweetheart." She would answer "Goodnight, Sweetheart". We repeated that many times until my sister told us to "Hush up and go to sleep."

My boyfriend Bobby visited me in Oklahoma while living with my sister, but when we had to say good-bye, I remember the oldest of my sister's children, Buster, saying to me, "Aunt Lillian, he won't get lost." He was only 5 years old at the time. It touched my heart how concerned he was for me. I was so in love with him, but he had to go to the bus station.

I was seventeen years old and taking care of my sister's three kids and a brand-new baby, and I was not happy. I felt like a live-in babysitter—which I was. I'm sure they needed me, but I was not happy with that situation. So, I made up a story to tell my sister, that I had had a dream that my grandmother who lived alone fell down the stairs, and she wasn't found for a couple of days. I said that I wanted to go live with her.

I had been working at the laundry at Fort Sill, the nearby army base in Oklahoma, and I'd saved up enough money for air fare for me to go to live with my grandmother in Maine. And so, I went and lived with my grandmother.

I learned a lot from my grandmother. She taught me a good work ethic; you do your best, work hard and don't complain. There was always encouragement, but you were to get up at 5:30 every morning; you were to go to work, no matter what. In fact, if you slept later than that, she would call and ask if you were going to sleep all day. If you didn't feel well, that was too bad. I don't remember being sick at Grams. I think it was because of all the antioxidants in the strawberries and blueberries we ate plus the fresh vegetables from her garden. We also ate venison for meat and fresh milk. I am very pleased that I had that opportunity to know her and to learn from her.

My grandmother, Lolie Powell, who I spent
summers with in Maine and my Aunt Evelyn

I visited Jr and Jean for a week or so but was sick the entire time. I spent most of the time on the couch and then it was time to go back to Grams. Immediately upon arriving, she said "make sure you get some good sleep, you have a job in the morning". She had gotten me a job in a chicken plant. It was the worst job I ever had in my life. They hung the chickens up on these racks, and as they passed by, my job was to take out the insides and put them in a pan. Gram would drop me off in the morning and pick me up at night, and after the first night I said, "Gram, I can't do this anymore." She said, "Well, try it one more day, and then if you can't do it, we'll get another job."

Well, the next day, I could not walk into the door. I just sat in the commons for the day until she picked me up. "I can't work there anymore," I said. And she said, "Well at least you got two days in." And I said, "No, one day." And she was not happy, but I worked for her, and then in the summertime, obviously, I did strawberries and blueberries.

Gram taught me a lot. She was also a teacher. She received a certificate from the State of Maine that she could teach in any public school in Maine for her life. I know for a fact she was a good teacher. Growing up, I didn't usually get things right away. It would take me a little while to get things, but when I got it, I got it. During the summer, Gram would teach me many things in a natural, talking tone. One I remember is how to add with nines. It was just a little trick—nine and four would always be one less than four – making it thirteen; nine and five would be always one less than five – making it fourteen.

Gram also taught me to regularly study the Bible and to regularly tithe. She taught me how to handle money. We were paid for our work in the blueberry and strawberry fields, and we were expected to give a tenth to the church, to spend some, and to save some. She would oversee our ledgers, and once in a while thirty-five cents would be missing from mine, and she would say, "Where is this?" Then I'd say, "Well, I must have put it in the church." And she'd point to the ledger and say, "No, this is over here." And I had to confess I was buying cigarettes. She was not happy with that fact.

I think God had his hand on her to teach me, because later on in my life, my husband left me with three kids, and I had to learn how to handle money. There was no choice; if we had nothing. I still knew that God would provide. I've written one short essay that describes Gram's house.

Gram's teaching certificate

Gram's House

By Lillian Martin

A quiet, peaceful country home in Liberty, Maine with the only neighbors of a small white church that held a maximum of 150 people down the road about 500 yards was very special because it was Gram's house. It was a large house with two enclosed porches, several bedrooms, a hayloft and garage. The house itself seemed to have warmth and kindness seeping through the walls. It felt good to hear only birds chirping, rooster crowing and the warmth of the sun shining through a window or a gentle breeze bringing the aroma of sweet peas, garden vegetables, and fresh fruit.

The front yard was always beautifully landscaped with carpet grass that was kept free of yellow dandelions which seemed to try to pop up now and again through the beautiful deep sea of green.

The mailbox at the edge of the road was positioned perfectly to the front door of the house. A path of smooth beautiful flat, round rocks were just far enough apart to make walking easy and broke into two paths to circle the tulips, gladiolas, and pansies. The paths again merged into one that led to the front door.

An area of the front porch was set apart for doing jigsaw puzzles with table and chair always set up. A small swinging door was provided for okay, the cat, to come out of the weather but only into the house when she was invited.

Window seats that stored toys, needlework items such as scrapes of material to make braided rugs were under each window on each side of the front door. In the center of the room was the shiny dinette table, always neatly cleared off, and chairs. To the left of that was the large black wood=burning stove. Beyond the stove was a door that lead to the back porch. It was a long screened-in porch that was used to store the portable washing machine, the buckets and containers used to shell garden peas and snap green beans or to prepare fresh cucumbers for the pickling by smoothing the stickers off. The satisfaction we got from these chores was not only that we were doing our part but in experiencing the fresh flavor of fresh vegetables at meal time. The smell of strawberries and blueberries cooking on the stove gave a mildly aroma that convinced us that it was not only delicious but good for us.
The cabinets, uniquely painted by using two different colors of brown and swirling the paint brushes, were located against the back wall of the kitchen storing pots and pans below the counter and dishes in the glass-door cabinet above the counter. Beside this the two foot rectangular sink contained one large bucket, kept full of well water, and one small basin used to wash hands and dishes. The drain went out the window to the back yard through a wooden trough. The refrigerator stood against the wall opposite to the wood-stove.

The doorway next to the wood stove lead into the garage. The stairs were directly connected to the wall adjacent to the kitchen. The stairs with the bedroom on one side and hay loft on the other side always creaked at the second to last stair. Before you reached the hay loft on your right, there was a small attic-like storage space that held a sea chest type trunk that clothes were stored in. Nothing was ever thrown away if they were usable.

I remember I had no shoes for church one Sunday but in that trunk was a pair my grandmother had worn that actually fi t my feet. The terrible thing about this was they were old-fashioned buttoned shoes. That was one of the most humiliating things I ever had to do.

On the shelves above this chest were several jigsaw puzzles, always tidy and neat, stacked precisely three boxes high. On the left of this storage space was the door that opened into the upstairs bedrooms.

The first one was filled with two beds. One was a day bed up against the front window. The second was a large poster bed that sat kitty-corner in the middle of the room with a large comforter and a home-made quilt laid across the bottom. Between the wall adjacent to the door and that bed was a large round hole about the size of a stove pipe in the floor. It was used to heat the bedrooms from the kitchen stove downstairs. Two more bedrooms were upstairs making it necessary to use six quilts on the farthest bed.

Gram's house was a very special growing environment. We learned not only how to work, be respectful (NO ONE talked back to Gram), but also that we should always be learning not only about the world and God but ourselves and who we are.

One night, in the middle of the night, I heard knocking at the door. I tried to wake Gram up, because we weren't supposed to answer the door without her. But I couldn't wake her up. I looked out my window, and it was Bobby. So, I tried to get down the stairs quietly. There was one stair that squeaked, and I knew to skip over it, so I got to the door quietly. When I opened the door, I said, "You can't come in here. Gram's supposed to answer the door." Well, I turned around, and there she was.

I told her who Bobby was, and she said, "Well, it's the middle of the night. You go up into this room and Bobby can go in that room and there'll be no shenanigans." So Bobby slept in the farthest bedroom. Mine was the next, and we did get a chance to do a little cuddling, but I wanted to be married in a white dress, so nothing happened.

The next morning, Bobby was expected to get up and work, like everybody else. I had to go to work in the blueberry fields of a neighbor, and I told him, "If you get hungry, the best thing to do is to tell Gram you like beans, 'cause she loves to make Boston baked beans in her wood stove. You can eat all you want. The rest of the stuff is kind of— you don't get as much—so if you need to get full, you say that."

Bobby was given chores around the house. He cut the tall grass with a sickle beside the house. I was out working in the field. When I got home, Bobby told me about the "small" lunch he had gotten. He said the piece of venison was about the size of a quarter. I asked why he didn't say he liked beans and he said "she didn't give me a choice".

I came home and we had supper, and we sat down at the kitchen table as we always did and read the Bible, and then I said, "Bobby and I want to get married." Gram said, "You're too young." I said, "But we wanna get married." And she said, "I'll give you a thousand dollars if you will wait a year." We looked at each other and we both said, "No. We're just going to hitchhike back to his mother's house in South Carolina." So we left Gram's and hitchhiked.

I never knew until I came back to Massachusetts in 2005, that an announcement was in the North Reading Transcript about our engagement. I am sure Jean did that. She always did things like that for other people. Her kindness always was evident.

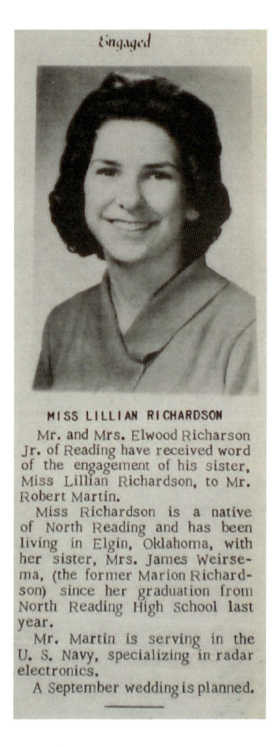

MISS LILLIAN RICHARDSON

Mr. and Mrs. Elwood Richarson Jr. of Reading have received word of the engagement of his sister, Miss Lillian Richardson, to Mr. Robert Martin.

Miss Richardson is a native of North Reading and has been living in Elgin, Oklahoma, with her sister, Mrs. James Weirsema, (the former Marion Richardson) since her graduation from North Reading High School last year.

Mr. Martin is serving in the U. S. Navy, specializing in radar electronics.

A September wedding is planned.

Engagement announcement

The first ride we caught was with a man in a truck, and Bobby stayed awake the whole time, 'cause he was protecting me. The truck driver went as far as he was going, and we found a Laundromat and we slept there. When I slept, Bobby was awake, and when Bobby was awake, I slept. We told everybody that we were married, even though we didn't have a ring. I'm sure most people knew that we weren't. Back in those days, it wasn't dangerous to hitchhike.

We stopped in Manchester, New Hampshire where his Aunt lived. He was not supposed to be off ship so he had to go back. I was living with his Aunt and heard stories of him and other girls and decided maybe it wasn't a good thing to get married so I called Jr and Jean and asked them to pick me up. His Aunt was a Beautician so I had her cut my hair real short. I was angry at Bobby and he liked my hair long.

About a week later, I saw Bobby again. I was riding in the car with Jean and told her I at least needed to talk to him. She let me go with him. I asked how did you get here again, I thought you weren't supposed to be off the ship. He said "I told them my girlfriend was pregnant". We talked and decided once again to be married. He said "you can believe me or believe what others say". I chose to believe him.

We went over to my brother's Junior and Jean's home and said that we were getting married. He said, "You're a fool to marry him," which made me cry. Bobby said, "Well, if you can't do that, then that's okay, and I'll just go." I said, "No, I want to go with you." So, I picked up a few of my belongings and we continued on our journey and went to his mother's trailer in South Carolina.

We told her that we were going to get married, and she said, "Well, you have to get married in a Catholic church." We had already discussed our beliefs, and I had asked him, "Do you believe that Jesus died for our sins and rose again?" And he said, "Yes." I said, "Well, I don't think we have a problem." So, when his mother said we had to get married in a Catholic church I said, "Well, that's fine. The beliefs that I have are the same as his. Some things are a little bit different, but the things that are important are not." So we set up a time to be married in a Catholic church.

Bobby's mother said, "Well, I'm not paying for anything, so you better go make some money." There was a circus going through town, and Bobby got a job. I don't remember what job he had there, but he wouldn't let me work. He made enough money for the priest, marriage license and my dress.

Before we got married, I slept on the couch and Bobby slept somewhere else. One night, I heard his mother crying. I went to ask her why she was crying, and she said, "I'm afraid that Bobby's gonna leave you." I said, "No, he's not gonna leave me." "Yeah, he's gonna leave you. Don't marry him." That didn't deter me, but in hindsight it was quite eye-opening.

I went to Goodwill and found a white dress for twenty-five dollars. His mother was a seamstress, so she made the dress fi t me good. I was thrilled how it looked. We were married November 19, 1964 in Charleston, S.C. with only his mother and sister in attendance. When we were saying our vows, a ray of sunshine came in through the window, and I felt like that was a blessing from God. We spent our wedding night in his mother's room.

My wedding day

After we got married, I found out that Bobby was AWOL again. He was stationed on the USS *Saratoga,* an aircraft carrier, and they said he had to go back immediately. Upon his return to the ship, he was put in the Brigg. I stayed with his mother.

I got a job in a mattress factory. It was my first job that wasn't obtained through family connections. It was very strange to hear bosses and employees swear at each other and me. Every day they would come in swearing at me, and I told my mother-in-law, "I really don't know if I can handle this." She said, "Well, that's okay. You don't have to work. You don't have to do anything." But I wanted to do my part to support myself until Bobby could come back and we could be together.

Being on an aircraft carrier, Bobby would go for nine months at a time then we would have some time together. He was stationed in Jacksonville, Florida. We got an apartment in Jacksonville, and we were able to stay together while he was in port. I never learned how to cook growing up but I tried the best I knew. The first meal was fried chicken (burnt on the outside and raw on the inside), lumpy mashed potatoes and corn on the cob that was tough to eat. He said it was delicious.

When Bobby came into port, he would have parties with his buddies. He thought it was more frugal to buy barrels of beer instead of buying the beer bottles, so he would buy two kegs of beer and they would party at the house, and then he would go back on the ship for nine months.

Well, our church was between our apartment and the place where we returned the kegs. I told Bobby not to worry about returning the empty kegs, because I could do that when he was gone. It would give me something to do—I kept complaining that I didn't have any kids or anything to do. I didn't even want him to pick up after himself, so I would have something to do while he was gone.

I remember trying to iron his uniform and it took a long time because I wanted it to be perfect. The sailor collar was especially hard. I ironed and ironed and still couldn't get the creases out of the collar. When he came in, he explained that it had to be creased like that to be regulation. He did not complain or make fun of me, he was always very kind.

I remember walking through the church parking lot, and the priest came out and saw me with an empty keg of beer. He knew who I was, and he said, "On your way back, why don't you stop by and we'll chit-chat a little bit." So I stopped by on the way back, and he says, "I just wanted to let you know that you can come over here and talk anytime you want. I know you might get lonesome when your husband's gone, and you might drink, and it might not be a good idea when your husband's gone."

I explained that the kegs were from the party that we had before Bobby went back onto the ship. The priest had a good laugh, and he said, "Well, I just wanted you to know that if you want somebody to talk to, that you can."

We didn't have much money but we liked to do things together. I wanted some canisters for the flour, sugar and tea. We made some together by painting coffee cans and putting decals on them. That was a very special time for us.

The next time Bobby came into port, we got another apartment where we could have a cat, so I had a cat to care for while he was gone. We wanted to have children, and we were trying and trying, but we were not able to. We tried for like, three years, and I still couldn't get pregnant. I would cry myself to sleep every night. I wanted to have a baby, and he said, "I do, too! I don't know what the matter is!" So finally he said, "I'm tired of this, I know what to do."

He brought home a bottle of wine. I don't like the taste of liquor or even beer, but while I was at his mother-in-law's home, she would drink some Manischewitz Concord grape wine, and I liked the taste. So, Bobby bought a bottle of that, and he poured half of it out and put Slow Gin Fizz in the other half. I drank the whole bottle that night, and they tell me I was pretty drunk. Evidently that did the trick, because nine months later, in September of 1967, Theresa was born.

We were really, really excited when we found out that we were pregnant. We wanted to tell Bobby's mom, so we drove from Jacksonville, Florida, to

Charleston, South Carolina, in a car that Bobby had just purchased. He hadn't bought insurance on it, and we were making payments.

We were driving in the middle of the night, and a horse was attracted by the headlights, evidently, and ran in front of the car. Back then there were no seat belts. I was sitting up on my knees next to Bobby, and when we hit the horse, I went forward and cut my head. They called the police. Somebody driving by made the remark, "Oh, the poor horse." That infuriated Bobby, because I was bleeding from the head, and he was worried about the horse. We waited for the police to come. The police said, "Well, you probably should go get that checked out."

We called Bobby's mother and stepfather, and they came and got us because the car had been totaled. That was the hardest payment to make each month on a car we no longer had. They thought I probably needed to get stitches. We went in the next day. The doctor was very unprofessional and said, "What did you do, just sober up?" I think we had waited too long for me to get stitches.

When we told Bobby's mother that we were pregnant, we were all excited, and the next time Bobby had to go out for his nine-month tour, we got an apartment near his mother in South Carolina, so that I would be there when the baby was born.

The baby was due September 20. On September 16, I was supposed to give Bobby's mom a perm, but I wasn't feeling that great, and so we agreed that I would do it another day. Then I started getting pains.

I was in labor, but the nurses said it was going to be a while, because it was my first. Bobby's Mom stayed with me the whole time I was in labor. I remember squeezing her hand. I found out later I put a sore on her hand where her ring was, because I squeezed so hard that it cut into her other finger.

Throughout the pregnancy, the doctor ordered no salt. I just got in the habit of using no salt and still use very little.

At one point they said, "We don't know if you're going to have complications, so we're going to put you under." It wasn't long compared to others I've heard about – she was born that night. I don't remember anything after that except waking up and being told, "You have a girl."

I actually wanted a boy first to watch over the others, 'cause I was going to have a whole lot of girls and wanted an older son to watch over the girls. We wanted twelve children, and I thought most of them were going to be girls. But I was thrilled to have her. Theresa was named after my mother-in-law.

After I got home from the hospital, Bobby's folks took me to their house. They said I needed to stay there, and I didn't like that. Bobby was out to sea. We couldn't get hold of him, but he finally did call on the due date, September 20. I had to pinch her so he would know that she had been born. I said, "You need to tell your mother that I can take care of the baby on my own at my own house." And so, I was allowed to go to our apartment and raise the baby.

Theresa was born in Charleston, but then we moved into a house in Summerville, South Carolina when Bobby got out of the Navy and began working for his mother in her Upholstery Shop. He worked as a salesman along with doing the upholstering, too. His mother had taught him as he grew up. A year and 3 months later, in December of 1968, Robert was born —we called him Bubba. Theresa could not say "Bobby" but she voiced "Bubba" and it stuck.

I had a false alarm with Robert. I went into the hospital with labor pains, but they sent me home. I was very discouraged. One of the nurses encouraged me with a simple statement: "I've never seen a pregnant woman that didn't have her baby." That helped a lot.

I didn't want Bobby to be there when the babies were born, because I didn't want him to see me hurt. And so he would drop me off at the hospital. He used to coach baseball for kids in the area, and while I was in labor with Bubba, Bobby was coaching a baseball game. I told him that I was going to name the baby after him

I'd never seen such a big smile on his face when I told him that the baby would have his name. He was very, very pleased with that. Yet, to get up at night if the kids were sick, or to give them a bottle, or to change their diapers, or to tend to them in any way was my job. Nowadays, that might be looked on as negative but not then. Bobby loved them, but he just wasn't involved in their everyday activities.

I didn't have a washing machine, and I had two in diapers. I remember telling Bobby one time when he came home from work, "You WILL buy me a washing machine." I washed cloth diapers in the bathtub and hung them out—two in diapers and pregnant with another one. It was quite a chore. But I tried to keep the house clean for when Bobby came home.

One Christmas he made me a corner sectional couch with stereo speakers in the arms. I loved it. He was very talented in the area of recreating things out of nothing. New couches out of frames and canisters out of coffee cans.

I remember one day, I had decided I was going to make sure the house was just perfect when Bobby came home. I had two toddlers and I was pregnant, and I worked all day long on the house, keeping it clean.

When he came through the door, I started crying. "I worked all day long to get this house to look nice by the time you got home, and it's just like you left it in the morning." He said, "Well, imagine what'd happen if you didn't do anything." He wasn't pressuring me. It was my idea to have things all straight.

Before Scotty was born, we moved into our own home he had gotten through a VA loan. It was a larger home with a big back yard.

We had Scotty August 11, 1970. He was very easy. We were real pleased, but then I began to think, *I'm not sure I can handle this anymore.* I was able to take care of them, but three of them were all I could handle. We thought we probably shouldn't have anymore—for a while, anyways. By the way, I did get my washing machine.

When Scotty was about to be born, I decided I didn't want to be at the hospital very long, so when labor started, I took the other two for a walk. I scrubbed the kitchen floor. I had an appointment with my doctor at seven o'clock that evening. When I went there, they took me straight to the hospital, and I had Scotty within an hour. They didn't have time to prep me, which was fi ne with me, 'cause I wasn't fond of that part of it. I was pleased he was born on his dad's birthday. Bubba had his name and Scotty had his birthday. I thought that they both would feel special.

I was pleased to see my son—another son. I thought for sure it was gonna be a girl. I had four girls' names picked out. I'm not sure how I came up with "Scotty," but Bobby agreed with it. I liked the sound of it.

Scotty was very, very cuddly, and I kind of babied him for a long time. I remember even when he was two, I would be carrying him, and Bobby would say, "He can walk, you need to put him down," but I was afraid that he was going to be my last one after expecting to be able to have twelve, so Scotty was a little bit more babied than the other two.

When Theresa was born, we were in the service. She cost twenty-five dollar, because there were too many births in September, so the government said I could choose a hospital and just pay twenty-five dollars. When Robert came along, the hospital bill was $250. By the time Scotty came along, it had doubled.

I kept telling Bobby that he needed to make payments, but he said his mother was going to pay the hospital bill, since he was working for her in her Upholstery shop. One day when she came over, I said—in front of Bobby—"Bobby says that you're going to pay the hospital bill for this baby." And she said, "No, I'm not." We confronted him, and so he started paying the bill, because I said I wasn't going to have the baby at home.

I have attached three children's stories that I wrote when I took a writing course in 1995. One was about Scotty when we went to my brother Charlie's funeral, and Scotty got lost and ended up in the orphanage.

Looking for My car

While visiting relatives in Manchester, New Hampshire, an incident that I will never forget happened.

My husband and I with our three children, Theresa 5, Robert 4 and Scotty 3 years old were visiting my husband's Aunt Cecile and Uncle Henry Desbeins in Manchester, New Hampshire.

My husband and I decided to go out for the evening visiting other friends that lived nearby. My husband's Aunt offered to care for our three children and we knew it was no trouble since by 6 p.m. they were all asleep anyway. Once they were asleep they never woke up till morning. Several tactics of mine made bedtime enjoyable for children, one of which was identical pajamas for the boys.

We were out until approximately about 3 a.m. and since the Desbeins had dogs that barked at any strange people, we went straight to our bedroom without checking on the children. This was one thing I never did even when we were at our own home but it seemed best for the entire household at the time.

Aunt Cecile woke us at 6 a.m. in the morning saying one of your children is missing.

"What!" we cried.

"I cannot find one of your children" the lady repeated.

As we frantically looked under beds and in closets in hopes he was just hiding, the other two were really beginning to feel the stress. We looked outside in the care literally everywhere. Finally, we realized we had to call the police.

Then my husband called the police and sure enough they had found a little boy wandering outside in the night. Scotty had wandered outside looking for us in this strange place. A neighbor spotted the child outside and called the police. The child was never afraid of policemen for he has always been taught that the policeman is your friend so it was no problem for the child to accept help from the policeman.

The officer drove up next to him and asked, "Where do you live?"

Scotty pointed down the end of the road, so the policeman asked him if he wanted to have a ride.

"Yes." Scotty said.

As he got in the police car, the policeman drove slowly to allow him to tell which house was his. Evidently, he was looking for our car. He did not find it. When the policemen got to the end of the street, he asked him again, "Where do you live?"

Scotty pointed to the other end of the street. So the policeman tried again to have him point out the house to no avail and ended up at the other end of the street.

Obviously, he was trying to find our car that was parked out front of the house when he went to bed.

So the policeman decided the child could not pick out his house and so arranged for him to be cared for at a nearby orphanage.

When my husband called the officers had information that a little boy was picked up on Cartier Street. They gave my husband the address of the orphanage and we loaded the other two children in the car and headed for the orphanage.

When we arrived at the orphanage, the house parents met us in the front of the orphanage and began asking us to provide proof that this child was ours. We were from Oklahoma and did not have a local address or telephone. We did not, of course, have a birth certificate for the child and could not prove that the child was ours. I was carrying Robert with the identical pajamas as Scotty had on. When the policemen who had picked up Scotty arrived and saw us, he said

"I see you have found him already."

"No, this is his brother Robert," I said

Then the house parents carried Scotty out to us, convinced only that it was ours because I had a child with the exact same kind of pajamas. Even so, I was expected to sign a paper saying were the legal parents of the child. By the time we left, they were satisfied that he was ours by Scotty's reaction to seeing us. He was calling us mom and dad so they were more convinced that he was our child.

This one tells when Scotty was born in 1970, the Hong Kong flu was in epidemic stage, and I gave the kids oranges for snacks. Everyone else around ended up getting Hong Kong flu, but the baby was fi ne, and none of my children got the flu.

Throughout the USA, the flu affects all of us. This true story from Charleston, S.C. teaches us an amazingly easy way to curb this communicable disease.

What will it be, fruit or cookies?

"Hurray! Summer is finally here!" exclaimed David as he got off the bus for the last time this year. Next year he enters the 1st grade. Theresa, Bubba, Jeff, Angie and Stacie were excited, too since now they can play all day instead of just half a day. Their back yards came together to make one big playground. Summertime was especially fun with riding toys, swing sets, sandboxes and of course, the tree house.

Theresa and Bubba Martin were sister and brother and they would soon have a new baby brother. Each child in the group was excited about a new baby in the neighborhood.

David said to Theresa, "I'll be the daddy and you be the mom."

"It's time for you to go to work, honey," Theresa said to David,

.

They hugged and kissed each other good-bye. As Daddy gave each one of the kids a good-bye hug, he told them each to be good for mommy today.

Theresa said to Bubba, "Go pick up the dirty clothes so we can wash them," and to Stacie, "Please run the vacuum in the living room."

Each had his own chores to complete. They did them with lots of enthusiasm.

"I'm glad about the new baby, aren't you? " Jeff said to Angie.

"I sure am, I can hardly wait." They hugged each other in excitement and went up to Mrs. Martin's house to talk more about the baby.

As they approached the front door of Theresa and Bubba's home, David comments, "Wow, what a big bag of oranges!"

"We have plenty, if you want some," Mrs. Martin said.

"It's about 10 o'clock now and that means what? She asked Angie.

"Snacktime!" they all cheered and ran to their houses.

Theresa and Bubba had oranges for snacks.

Bubba asked, "Why do we have fruit for our snacks when other kids have sweets?"

As Mom sat down with them, eating an orange herself, she explained, "Fruits and vegetables are part of the four food groups. You will learn in school that your body needs fruits and vegetables to grow strong and healthy. Fruits like oranges have Vitamin C that is very helpful in fighting off colds. How many times have you been sick this year?" she asked Bubba.

He thought for a minute and said, "Just one time, when I hurt my knee," "That was an accident, it wasn't really a sickness", explained mom.

"We don't get colds or flu very much because we eat fruits that fight off the sicknesses." Mom continued.

Bubba said, "Can I have another orange?"

Mom said, "Sure, you can eat all you want." She went on to say, "When you eat sweets, you must limit them when you do have them. You need room for the food that helps your body grow. It's also good for me because I have a baby in my belly. I need to stay healthy so the baby will be healthy too. What I eat goes right to the baby and either helps him grow or hurts him."

Finally, the baby arrived on August 11, 1970. The children were so excited when Mrs. Martin brought him home. Mrs. Martin was very proud of her baby and each of the children was included in the excitement of visiting and seeing the baby.

Angie, seeing Mrs. Martin's worried look as she watched the children as they played, asked, "Aren't you happy about the baby anymore?"

"Oh, I sure am, but there's a flu going around that is real serious and I'm afraid the baby will get it, "she told her.

The very next day, Angela's brother came by to say that Angela had the flu. Terry was sad because she knew it was not fun to be sick.

Next day, Stacie's mom came by to say Stacie also had the flu. David and Jeff came down with it too. Theresa and Bubba now had no one to play with and the baby slept almost all the time, so they were sad.

Mrs. Martin really was worried now since her husband had heard on the news that the Hong Kong Flu was in epidemic stage. It was spreading faster among older people and little babies simply because their immune system is fragile.

The young because of their rapid growth rates creates an increased demand for nutrients and the old because the immune system simple deteriorates with age. (The Complete Book of Vitamins from the editors of Prevention Magazine.) Time passed and so did the flu epidemic.

Something very amazing happened. Not one person in the Martin household got the fl u. Mrs. Martin was extremely happy with her healthy baby. Mom explained to the children how the oranges they ate acted like a medicine to keep them from getting sick. The snacks containing mostly sugar did not have vitamins that their bodies needed to help protect them from diseases. Oranges contain Vitamin C that fights off colds personally experienced by Kenneth Cooper, M.D., fitness expert and author of <u>The Aerobics Program for Total Well Being</u>, and even fought off the Hong Kong Flu in this family.

Another story that I wrote was "Where's the Purple Cow?" which is about an incident that happened while living at the trailer on 8000 B Wynne Lane in Austin, Texas.

Where's the Purple Cow?

By Lillian Martin

Some stories are true and some are not. One purple cow story I know is not true but another I happen to know is true. Listen to this story and you decide.

"Listen to that!" exclaimed Jimmy as he coat caught the stack of marbles collected by Joey and scattered all over the moung.

"Listen to what?" Joey said angrily. "You are just making something up because you don't like me winning."

"Hear the moaning coming from the bushes?" Jimmy continued as if nothing else was said.

"All I hear is a poor loser." Joey said.

"I hear it." Jenny said.

"Oh, great, now you are taking sides." Joey said disgustedly.

"No, listen, you nerd, it's coming from over there." Jimmy said pointing to the trees. As they listened again, a low moaning sound came from just the other side of the trees in their backyard. It was a soft, sad eerie sound like something out of a scary movie, "Go ahead and go, "Jenny said, "I don't like scary things." So the boys began walking toward the sound. With Jimmy leading, they crept closer and closer.

"Wait for me!" Jenny cried. The boys didn't even bother to turn around. All of a sudden, Jimmy darted backwards.

"Wow!" he shouted, "There's a live animal in that big hole!" They all walked closer to get a better look. "Gross!" cried Jenny

"He's stuck", Joey said almost crying. "Help me pull him out."

"No, Joey, we can't do that. He's too big and slippery from all that mud he's stuck in." Jimmy advised.

"Well, we have to help him, he sounds like he's hurting!" Joey sobbed.

"We will, "Jimmy reassured him, "But we need some help. First let's tell mom…" Before Jimmy could say anymore, Joey was running back to the house to get mom.

"Mom!" Joey cried. "There's a purple cow in the big hole in the yard!"

"Now, Joey", mom said still with the phone to her ear, "for one thing there's no hole in the yard and you know there's no such thing as a purple cow. Remember after we read that story last week I explained that there was no such thing and you said you understood?"

"I'm talking long distance to grandma, don't you want to say hi to her?" she asked.

"Hi, grandma, I'm fine." Joey said, "Mom doesn't believe in purple cows. I bet you do, huh grandma?" His face lit up as he turned to face his mom.

"See, grandma believes me!" Joey said grinning.

"Go outside and play." Mom said lovingly.

He handed the phone back to his mom and ran back outside.

"Well, where's mom?" Jimmy asked.

"She didn't believe me!" Joey said. The expression on his face turned to concern again as he saw the animal still stuck.

"I guess WE are going to have to convince mom." Jimmy said to Jenny.

They started back to the house with Joey still watching the animal with so much compassion, he seemed to hurt himself.

"Remember, Joey, don't try to pull him out yourself." Jimmy advised. "Don't get near enough to touch him either. His is hurting and might not understand that you are trying to help and he could hurt you."

As Jimmy and Jenny approached the house, mother was standing in the doorway.

"Mom, please come see what we found, there's an animal that needs our help." Jenny said.

"Is this the purple cow Joey was talking about?" Mom asked.

"Well, yes, but it's not purple but it looks that way to Joey." It's an animal stuck in a sewage hole that someone must have left the cover off." Jimmy explained.

"Oh, my goodness, did you leave Joey with the animal?" Mom asked as she rushed down the stairs toward the children.

"Yea, mom, let's hurry. Joey is really sad about it" Jenny said.

"We can't lift this calf out but Mr. Matthew's pick-up truck might be able to do it if he had a rope." Jimmy said.

"That's a good idea." Mom replied.

"Can I go with you, Jimmy?" asked Joey

"You'll have to keep up with me; I'm going to run fast." Jimmy replied.

It was only a few minutes later that Mr. Matthews and the boys arrive in his pick-up truck. Looking over the situation, Mr. Matthews explained, "I'm afraid I can't help, my truck can't fi t between those trees." He said turning away. "Find out who the animal belongs to and let them worry about it!"

"Wait!" Jimmy said. "This is a live animal; you can't just leave him there!" Jimmy said now very upset.

"I'm sorry, it'll take a tractor maybe to pull that animal out." Mr. Matthews said.

"I know someone who has a tractor, will you take me there? He lives down the next street." Jimmy said.

"O.K." Mr. Matthews said, "But I'm not going to be responsible for that calf."

Before long the tractor arrived. As Jimmy jumped off the tractor, mom said smiling, "Hi, Mr. Hack, can you believe they found a purple cow today?"

"Well, let's see what we can do for this purple cow." Mr. Hack replied. "Jimmy you go get the rope in the back of the tractor and Joey, you start moving these limbs out of the way so I can back the tractor up to the very edge of the hole." Mr. Hack instructed.

The children did as they were instructed. Mr. Hack carefully put an old rug under the rope before wrapping around the calf's body. He then asked Jimmy to get into the tractor, put it in gear and gently press the gas.

"Are you sure you want him to do that?" mom asked.

"Sure, he'll be fi ne" was Mr. Hack's reply.

Jimmy gladly did as he was told.

"Press harder, Jimmy," Mr. Hack shouted as he and several men grabbed the animal trying to guide him out.

"We're going to have to use a harness because it can't seem to help us." One of the neighbors commented.

As they put the harness on, once again Mr. Hack gave Jimmy orders to put his foot on the gas slowly but firmly. Jimmy did what he was told to do.

"Just a little bit more," Mr. Hack instructed. "There, he is up, a little shaky but he's out." The calf was lovingly cared for by children and adults alike.

Joey was so proud of his brother. They all shared in their accomplishment without noticing how muddy and slimy they all had gotten including Jenny.

"I bet this calf belongs to Mr. Brown." Mr. Hack said. "May I use your phone, Mrs. Martin?"

"Of course" Mrs. Martin replied.

In a few minutes Mr. Hack approached the children who were still stroking the calf and told them that the owner was on the way.

"What's going to happen now?" Joey asked very concerned.

"Well, I imagine the owner will give him a bath and make sure he is o.k."
"Very soon a trailer pulled up and Mr. Brown got out of his truck. Mr. Hack told him the whole story.

"Thank you, children for getting help for my calf. You are all good neighbors." Mr. Brown told them acknowledging everyone there.

"If you will help me get him up into the trailer I will take her home and have her checked out by the vet and get her all cleaned up.

I think we all should complain to the city for leaving a cover off that sewer. If one of you children fell into that hole, you wouldn't be as luck as my calf was."
He said sternly.

"Oh, my, " mother said. "You are so right!"

"O.K. children, now who is the fi rst to the bathtub?" Mother asked.

"Jimmy!" cried Jenny and Joey. "After all he is the hero of the day.

Scotty was more emotional than the other children—in a good way. He was very kind and caring, and he could kind of change my mind with his puppy eyes.

My daughter was a very, dainty girl who always liked to stay clean and is a perfectionist, very special. Therefore, she is an excellent gardener and artist. She had to look beautiful each time she left the house. At one point we had to set up a corner of the living room with a mirror, etc. so the rest of us could use the bathroom.

Bubba wanted to take care of things. In fact, when his dad left, he felt like he should take care of us and protect us. When he was younger, he had a paper route that helped us out a lot, and he worked at Whataburger and brought home the extra food. He had an unfortunate encounter on the paper route since he was out at 3 a.m. each day. He continued on into other odd jobs.

When James Bouland left us and Bubba knew we had no money, he made a wrong choice and ended up in trouble with the law. The law came down really hard on him and he had to pay lots of money and in that process he attained a good work attitude. He is a very good worker, a sort of perfectionist. He does his jobs well.

When Bobby left us the first time, I called my sister in Lawton, Oklahoma, and the kids and I went to live with her for a while. We took a Greyhound bus from Summerville, South Carolina to Lawton, Oklahoma. Bubba thought it was fun to sit on the back seat because it bounced up and down when the bus driver went over bumps. Soon he became car sick. I called my sister, who had trained to be a nurse and she suggested I get some Dramamine. That did the trick and we got there safely.

Bobby came back there and we were reunited. Bobby, Marion and Jim opened an upholstery shop together. Marion was an excellent seamstress and Bobby knew how to run a shop. That did not last very long.

When they went out of business, Uncle Jim got another job, and then Bobby got a job working at a gas station in nearby Apache, Oklahoma.

The owner had two gas stations, and so I ran one and Bobby ran the other. Our boss allowed us to live in a house behind the gas station where I worked. The kids were in school all day. They were quite young— they attended head start, kindergarten and first grade.

While we were living there, we had a cat—a momma cat. There was a field between the gas station and the house, and momma cat went out into the field and got a mouse and brought it to her babies. It was in a contained area, so that they could learn how to catch a mouse. She went into the field, caught a mouse, and then stood up on the top of the stairs where they were and let the mouse go. She was teaching her little children how to get the smell of mice.

It was an exciting adventure for the kids. They really enjoyed that. They always loved animals.

Theresa had several cats. One was named Ashes, and to this day, she has a cat.

Thomas was really into dogs. He always wanted a dog. A lot of times we couldn't have one, because we had apartments, but one day he came home and said he found a stray dog. It was an Irish Setter and a really friendly dog. I said, "He must belong to somebody." We couldn't find a tag on him or any indications of who his owner was. Thomas convinced me to keep him for a little while, but so I said, "Only until we can find the owner."

That dog ended up sleeping on the bed with me, which was fi ne. I found out later that Thomas had taken off the identification tags, because he wanted to keep the dog. He has one now that he is grown, and he really enjoys dogs.

While we were living in the house in Apache, Oklahoma and I was working at the gas station, we had a 150-pound St. Bernard who took me for a walk. This was in a country setting, back in the day when customers did not pump their own gas. Sometimes I would only pump one gallon of gas for a customer. The same customer would come back the same day for another gallon of gas. Back then it cost 35 cents a gallon. The little store was small—it just had Coke and candy near the register, but of course I would have to leave that to go out and pump gas.

One time, I was pumping gas and I'd left Sam, the St. Bernard, inside, behind the counter. All of a sudden, two of the guys who'd gone inside were trying to get through the door at once, and two others jumped out the window. Evidently, they had gone close to the cash register, and Sam had jumped up on the counter with his front paws and said, "Woof." It was very comical to see them so scared, trying to get away from him.

I told my husband the story when he returned home from working at his gas station. I don't think it was a good decision, but Bobby decided to put Sam in training. I was told that you aren't really supposed to do that with St. Bernards, but Bobby felt like the training would make Sam a better protection for me.

When Sam came back from training, he seemed a little bit different, but at first he was okay. A lot of times my husband and the children would roughhouse on the bed, and the dog would be involved. During one of these play sessions, Sam suddenly attacked Scotty. Scotty's face was inside of the dog's mouth, and there were teeth marks on both sides of his face.

Bobby was right there to get Sam off Scotty, but we could not take the chance that it would happen again while we were not close by so we had to find another home for Sam away from children. I thought it was because Sam was trained to be a guard dog, or maybe he became jealous of Scotty or perhaps was accidentally hurt somehow during the play time. I really don't know the reason.

It was near Christmas of 1977 when Bobby left us for good. We were in Austin, Texas. He ran two Upholstery Shops and doing well. They were Alex Acosta Upholstery and Economy Upholstery He was involved with franchising merchandise in Mexico and said he was going to make a trip there. Each day he would call and ask how much I deposited as I was working as secretary for the Alex Acosta Upholstery shop. I told him. Each day he would withdraw that amount. He borrowed money from our salesman and then he was gone without paying the payroll. I did not realize he was not coming back until one of the workers opened my eyes to the fact he had a girlfriend. We left the trailer we were living in. We were buying from it from Mr. Acosta and I knew I could not make payments on it. At first, the kids and I stayed at the Salvation Army, but we could only stay for three days. Then that salesman that Bobby borrowed money from and did not repay put us up in a hotel.

My four children

We had nothing. The first night, we had bubble gum for supper. Then I got some bologna and sandwich bread and put it on the bureau at the hotel. The welfare gave us emergency food stamps till we could get paperwork done and in an apartment. During the night, a rat got in it, so we all stood on the bed and told Bubba he needed to get rid of it, which he did.

After talking to the welfare people, they got us an apartment but it was in an all-black neighborhood. The children had to attend an all-black school. They were the only 3 white children in the school. Scotty did not understand the commotion he caused by chanting in the halls – "I'm a honkey, I'm a honkey, ain't that great?" One day he came running home to say that some boys had Theresa trapped behind a dumpster. Bubba was there trying to protect her. I am not very assertive but the mother in me marched right down there and with the meanest expression on my face I could muster I told them they better get home. I was very surprised when they did because that's not me. I believe that was God again, our protector.

A couple in the Big Brothers program came by to interview me so that the boys could have a "big brother." The couple took one look at where we were and said, "You don't need to be here." They immediately took us into their home, until I could gather enough money to get the trailer that I finally did find. I could only help with food by using the food stamps I got from the welfare. They had children, too and they all seemed to get along well. They did not want any money. This was another obvious provision from God. I was able to save the unemployment money and look for something for us to live in.

When I found the trailer, I didn't tell the landlord I had three kids, because it only had two bedrooms. When I moved in and he saw that there were three kids, I thought I was in big trouble, but God was gracious, and the landlord just said, "Well, you can't leave them in the streets." It was a roof over our head and God's provision for us.

The trailer was two miles from the nearest bus stop to search for a job so the welfare department said I didn't have to look for a job because we were in a "remote" area. However, I wanted more for my children.

My friend Joyce with husband Leroy - friends for over 30 years

We had no car, and I couldn't drive. Bobby had never let me drive. Before I got a job, and able to buy a car, we would all go to the grocery store together when we got food stamps and all carry the groceries back to the trailer. Scotty was very demonstrative, and if a car was passing us, he'd turn around and give a sad face. They would end up picking us up and giving us a ride. These were hard times for the children but those experiences made them very strong.

I met another one of my best friends, Joyce Young, when we first moved into the trailer. I didn't know the area, and I was living on unemployment, and the form showing the places I had searched for a job had to be mailed every week or I would not get paid the small amount that I did get. I was walking down the road looking for a post office. Joyce pulled up and asked if I needed a ride somewhere and I told her I was new in the area and looking for a post office. She said. "Get in, and I'll drive you around."

Well, we didn't find a post office, and she had to go somewhere, so she dropped me back at trailer, but she took the mail with her, promising to mail it for me. I thought afterwards, "Oh goodness, I messed up big time." But Joyce has turned out to be a very, very special friend over the thirty-five years that I've known her. She was Theresa's "big sister" in the Big Brothers program. The trailer did not have a washer or dryer and she noticed that and offered hers for me to use. She even provided the soap as at first I didn't have anything but food stamps. I really needed a phone because the kids had to come home after school alone. Even after I got a job, she paid the deposit for us to be able to have a phone. It was a great help!!

A neighbor, James Coleman was very good to us. He cut the grass, took the kids fishing and helped us out with food. I was very naive and ended up becoming intimate with him. I got pregnant and let him move in because I thought we would get married. He was involved in the household activities and a very good cook. However, once he was going to spank Theresa for not washing the dishes as she was told on her bare butt, I said, "No, you're not." He slapped my face and I told him he better not do that again, but he did. When I ran to get the phone, he pulled it out of the wall, so I told the kids to go outside somewhere. I told James to go and not come back. I was only a few months pregnant. He said "You can't have that baby without me". To which I replied "Watch me!" We were attending Bannockburn Baptist Church where Frank Deutsch was counseling Scotty and the entire family.

Frank Deutsch was very instrumental in giving a boost to our faith. When I got pregnant with Thomas, we were going to Frank's church, because he had counseled all of us. When I got pregnant with Thomas I told the children. Scotty felt a closeness to Frank so much so that he said, "Guess what? My mom's going to have a baby." Well, Frank knew that my husband was gone, but never once did I feel condemned; never once was I looked upon as second-class. In fact, Frank and his wife helped me tremendously during that time. They even took care of the three teenagers while I was in the hospital having Thomas.

We didn't have furniture. We were sleeping on the floor in the low rent housing after providing them with the information that Bobby had served in the service.

That fact put us on the top of the list as housing became available. Frank and friends from the church provided a lot of the furniture for us. I felt more unconditional love through Frank and through Bannockburn Baptist Church in Austin Texas than all through my life. I learned how to accept something given to me, then.

I had always felt that if I made a mistake, then the consequences were my responsibility and nobody else's. Thomas's father's name was James Coleman. I had allowed him to live with us because I thought we were going to get married. He only lived with us for a short time. After the incident with Theresa and his tearing the phone out of the wall, I told him that the children and I were going to leave the house for a while, and he could take whatever he wanted while we were gone, but to leave and not come back. When he left, he took the blankets among his belongings.

One time when I was in Frank's office I had a cold, and he asked what was wrong. I said, "Well, when James left, he took the blankets." The next day, when I came home from work, a brand new blanket had been delivered. The kids had to be home by themselves after school, because I didn't have the money to pay for after school care, so I asked Scotty who brought the blanket by. I was upset because Frank had brought the blanket. In my way of thinking, it was not his problem. He shouldn't have to buy something because I had a child.

I called him up and said, "You shouldn't have done that." He very frankly told me, "I'll do whatever God tells me to do." That helped me begin to learn to accept help from other people, but it was not easy for me. It was very hard to accept help, when I felt like I should do it myself. That was quite a stressful time, but God was teaching me a valuable lesson.

Frank Deutsch with the soup kitchen crew feeding the homeless

Our first family photo

Frank became a very dear friend. He counseled Scotty and gave him the support he needed. Scotty felt like his dad left because of him, because Bobby really took a shine to Bubba because he was athletic, while Scotty was more into books. Actually, the whole church gave the support that we all needed.

Along with being associate pastor at the church, Frank operated a soup kitchen for the homeless in the middle of the city of Austin. We were proud to help him serve meals to the homeless and help him anyway we could.

The children all loved Tommy when he was born. Frank Deutsch and his wife, Centra took care of my three teenagers while I was in the hospital delivering Thomas. Theresa, Bubba and Scotty really, really fell in love with the baby. I had lots of help with Thomas, compared to when the older three were growing up. I'm honestly not sure how much I took care of Thomas, because the children wanted to take care of him a lot.

One miracle associated with Thomas's birth happened when I was a couple of months pregnant. Before James left and was looking for work, he would drive me to work and then go look for work. As I said, I was a couple of months pregnant, and we got hit by a cement truck. We totaled the car, but we weren't hospitalized or anything. We were just shook up.

The doctor monitored things for a long time, and said the baby was all right. When it came time for Thomas to be born, my water broke at like three o'clock in the morning. Thomas wasn't born until one o'clock in the afternoon, and the nurses were concerned, because they said I had an extremely large amount of water in the sac. When they heard about the accident, they said that it was God's way of protecting Thomas—that there was trauma at the very beginning of my pregnancy, and my body automatically made extra fluid to protect the baby from any more harm. I think that was God's doing, also.

I was thirty-five years old when I learned how to drive. That was after Bobby left. An elderly neighbor while we lived on Wynne Lane named Mr. Hack showed me how to drive. He was very helpful when I first moved into the trailer too. We didn't have food for supper until I got my first paycheck. I was paid monthly. The kids got free lunches at school, but we didn't have money to buy groceries to make supper with. Mr. Hack brought over chicken several nights for us to have for supper.

I told him that, once I started working, it was very important for me to try to save up to get a car. He said, "Once you start, once you find a car, let me know and I'll teach you how to drive." And he did. I was surprised. The Pinto was an automatic which proved much easier for me than a standard.

Mr. Hack was very patient with me and took me out to practice and told me exactly what to do, and the first time I went for the license, I got it. I studied the book and then went and got the license. I didn't pass the parallel parking part, but they passed me anyway. I still can't parallel park, but that's okay.

When I first drove a car, I was extremely nervous, and the children had to not say a word for the whole trip. After I got my license and the car, we were driving to Lewisville, Texas to visit my sister and I saw a cow on the side of the road, and we pulled over, because I wanted to take a picture of it. When the picture was developed, there was no cow. I had missed the mark. So that became a family joke.

Mostly I loved to have family portraits made. Our first one was free. The company was trying to sell packages and offering a free one. Since we didn't have any money, I just took the free one.

When Tommy was three years old, I married James Bouland, a man I met at work. It didn't last too long, I divorced him; after hearing he showed Tommy how to do drugs.

We were married 10 years but didn't live together much as he would become angry and leave for long periods of time. Three months after we were married, he wanted to go on a picnic for Mother's Day and I wanted to go to church. We had an argument and he called me a "Rotten Mother!". It hurt me to the core. He left again and I dropped the kids off at church and spent the morning walking the railroad tracks crying. I was trying to be the best mother I could be and it really upset me. I wonder if my choice of comfort came from remembering going to work with my father and waiting on the railroad tracks for him.

James worked as a tow truck driver. He said we needed to move to North Austin because his work was closer and he didn't want to attend church because Bannockburn Church was my church not his. He said he would go to another church and I wanted us to go together. That did not happen but we did move when Theresa graduated high school. At that point the children and I attended Anderson Mill Baptist Church. We had lots of different values. He brought X rated movies for the kids to watch and I could not understand why. I remember one day being so upset when I came home for lunch from work that I could not stop crying and couldn't go back to work that day. He left saying he couldn't handle the teenagers but several years later came back when only Thomas was home and he then had problems with him.

When he left we had to move because I could not afford the rent. The Anderson Mill Baptist Church was so helpful. It was close to Christmas and Thomas had asked for a "Teddy Ruxpin", and I assured him he couldn't have one but one of the members of that church did give him one. He was a delighted youngster.

When Tommy started growing up, the other three were leaving home. He was an awesome child growing up, but when the other three began to leave, he felt like they were abandoning him. He didn't like being an only child.

We began attending Great Hills Baptist Church and I began teaching again. I taught 2nd grade Sunday school for several years. Here is where I met Mark Weaver. His daughter, Rebecca was in my class. I would ask for prayer requests and she would ask prayer for her father because he was in jail. Some children didn't understand but he was a great advocate for the unborn and would help girls make a decision not to have an abortion. So during demonstrations, he would have to go to jail. Tommy made his profession of faith at Great Hills and was baptized. The other three had made their professions of faith at Bannockburn Baptist Church within 8 months from when we started attending.

Thomas was very, very smart in school but ended up getting in some trouble, because the teachers didn't challenge him. He got into drugs and ended up in a juvenile jail. He had not gone to high school at all, and they asked me if it was all right to give him the GED, and I said fi ne, that that would be good.

Tommy took the GED and passed it the first time, without any high school. That just confirmed what I had always thought—that instead of challenging him, they just labeled him "trouble."

Tommy had a rough time for a while, but I am very pleased to say I am very, very proud of him right now as an adult. I enjoy talking to him and hearing what he is doing.

As he grew, Thomas related more with Bubba. He and Bubba hit it off, because Bubba got in trouble, too and they could relate to each other. Bubba helped him get jobs at an apartment complex as a repairman where Thomas learned a lot. While Thomas was staying with Tom and Rowena Stenis, he and Bubba worked together to replace an air-conditioning system.

Tommy and Bubba

Now that he's grown up, Thomas is an excellent house remodeler and does landscape also. He does floors and tile and has remodeled a house for one of his friend's parents. That was a really, really sad situation. This man's twenty-something-year-old daughter hung herself, and three months later, the wife jumped off a bridge. There were two suicides in the family, and the father and son asked Thomas to come and redecorate, to redo the house so that they could go on with their life. It was very, very hard. Thomas was very instrumental with helping this man cope with the losses. I was extremely proud of his compassion. Thomas has always had compassion for older people. Thomas is only thirty-two, and this other man is in his fifties, but he told me that he wouldn't know what he would have done without Thomas. Thomas put new hardwood floors and cleaned the house that required major cleaning and remodeled it.

My three sons

Because the man was unemployed Thomas has rented out all the rooms to cover the mortgage and the utilities. I went to see Thomas, because he was having trouble being able to see his daughter, and I just had to tell him, "I couldn't do what you are doing. You have a very special gift of compassion toward people who are grieving," and I was just really impressed with his compassion.

My Christian journey started the first time I went to a Billy Graham crusade; it was not long after I my mother had died. Billy Graham preached that it doesn't matter if you go to church or how many Bible verses you know, if you have not accepted Jesus Christ into your life and asked him to forgive your sins, you're not going to heaven.

I thought, "Wow, he is talking to me!" I sang in the choir; I knew lots of Scripture; I helped in the Sunday school; I even sang solos, but I wasn't there in that belief. I had not been confronted with that. So I went down and I accepted Christ as my Savior. I knew that my mother was in heaven, and at that point that was probably a deciding factor. I've grown to realize that Jesus is the reason that my mother is in heaven. That's how God used that situation.

I grew tremendously at while attending Bannockburn, Great Hills and New Hope Churches.

Theresa and me teaching Sunday school

I made several trips to Romania through New Hope Church. Pastor Mark Weaver is the pastor of this church, and he was having short-term mission trips to Romania. The first time I met Alisa, my best friend, she and Pastor Mark Weaver were planning a mission trip to Romania, and Alisa said, "You've got to go with us, because I'm the only girl on the trip, and I want you to go with me." So I thought about it. My daughter's comment when she first heard about it was "no, she's not going that far away." but, the Lord indicated I should go and that was what I did. My daughter did get used to the idea.

Pastor Mark asked me if I would be interested in going to Romania. I wasn't so sure about it. My daughter, Theresa said "My mother doesn't go that far". I met Alisa and she was the only female that was going and she asked me to think about it, too. So I decided that would be okay. We had to come up with money for the trip but the church had car washes and garage sale and special people like Fil and Melba Hendrix contributed and soon I had the amount needed. We had to wear long skirts because of the culture there so we got together what we needed.

Letter I wrote to Pastor Mark after my 1st trip to Romania in 1998:

> Mark, I 'm sorry I can't be there Sunday. My sister-in-law passed away Thursday in Boston. She had diabetes and it just got too much for her heart. She is a believer. My brother and her have been married for 50 years. Please pray for them and their 7 children and their families. We all
> loved her so much.

About Romania –

If you would express my appreciation to the congregation for their prayers, I would be most grateful. Please emphasize to them that their prayers were vital and God moved because they were praying so they are just as important as those of us who physically went.

You prayed for me to be able to lead someone to Christ and He answered. It was so awesome. She is a 12-year old girl who came to the meetings. Before the meeting on Wednesday, July 1, 1998, she came to me and was asking me something in Romanian. I hugged her and she moved back into the crowd of children. A few minutes later she was back obviously asking me something again. I called for an interpreter and asked him to ask her what she was saying. The interpreter said she wants to know where to go to find God. "Wow!" So I tried to take her and sit down privately to talk but the other kids just kept following us. So I finally told an interpreter to tell the other kids if they wanted to stay, they had to be real quiet while I talked to Roxanne. They were quiet and listened as Roxanne repented of her sins and accepted the Lord. I gave her a Romanian Bible and on the last day I told he it was our last day and as she stuck out her bottom lip in disappointment, I could not help but cry. I had the interpreter write down in Romanian what I wanted her to do. I told her to read her Bible every day. Pray every day. Attend either a Pentecostal or Baptist church there in Teccuci. I asked if her parents would let her do that, and she said yes. The last day was very emotional with her clinging to me all the way to the car. I kissed her and told her "I love you: In English, she told me. "I love you, too". It was totally awesome.

Obviously, that was the highlight but God did so much more. I stayed with a couple who were so sensitive to the spirit. It was nothing for them to say. We will pray- and that meant we all knelt in the middle of the living room floor. I couldn't understand a word they were saying but that didn't matter. It was awesome. I have never been so blessed. One day it rained in Teccuci so my shoes were muddy and since you take off your shoes before going into the houses in Romania, mine were at the door during that night. The lady of the house got up during the night and washed my shoes. That experience was so humbling, I was speechless.

The Romania Christians sing praises and you are sure you are already in heaven. We would travel one hour each day to Teccuci and sing praise songs on the way. They are some of the same songs we sing. We would sing them in English and they would sing them in Romania. Their voices had such a sound it sounded like 5 Jennifers. I couldn't help but tell Don-it doesn't get any better than this and he agreed.

Obviously, there were lots more that happened in a week but I will be most happy to share to anyone who asks and again I would like to thank all those who prayed for us. The people that went and those who prayed made up a team that God used mightily and I am so thankful I was able to be a small part. Love, Lillian

Roxanna and me in Romania - 1st one I lead to the Lord

I was fifty-three years old at that time, and I had never led another person to Christ. The first person I lead to Christ was Roxanna, a twelve-year-old girl in Romania.

I made several other trips after that.

Romania 2001

Our verse this year was from the New Living Translation Matthew 28: 19-20

Therefore, go and make disciples of all nations, baptizing them in the name of the Father and the Son and the Holy Spirit.

Teach these disciples to obey all the commands I have given you and be sure of this: I am with you always, even to the end of the world.

God did some awesome things this year because of your prayers. I want to thank you and hope make you realize how important those prayers were and are.

We had no major trouble in traveling, no one had any significant health problems even though we were always busy, we had physical strength to complete our week's work. Many new Christians and many were encouraged.

As you know a request of mine was to lead (I expressed especially to the 10 prayer partners that signed my commitment) 4 children to Christ. I have their pictures and names and address for Mary, Maxine, Brenda and Jada who were in my Experiencing God Class that expressed an interest in discipling them by sending letters and gifts to them. I led one little boy to Christ the first of the week and on the last day (didn't realize I would lead the other 3 that day) before the service I was impressed by a 12 year old girl named Christina who took care of her 5 year old brother to get her address to take home to pray because she was listening and participating in the activities – I saw a remarkable change in her countenance but she was not saved. That night she was one of the three who wanted to ask Jesus into her heart. Two little girls also said they wanted to ask Jesus into their heart but they were not ready because when I asked them if they had done anything wrong (sinned) they said no, so please pray but God is drawing them but this is His business. They each are eight years old but they were so petite they looked around 5 years old. They often didn't have shoes to wear and the same clothes most of the week. In Fundeanea we had lots of activities for children. We showed the Jesus fi lm at the house. The family continually ministers to neighbors with food and love. The children were there early in the morning and wanted to be around us as long as possible. One boy (12 years old is the head of his house. His father died in an accident that put a knife through his leg and he bled to death.

He is trying to help his mother support him and four brothers. He was very hungry one night after working in the field. This house is an oasis to these children. Mihaela is teaching the children at Ochanca and she assisted me. Such a beautiful lady inside and out. We played games with the children and you could see the love she had for them. We also got close = I went to her home and had a traditional Romanian meal – rice, meat mixed with egg and rolled in a grape leaf. She is married to Lucio and such a great couple they are.

Another VERY specific prayer was answered that we would find Roxanne. We didn't tell her we were coming and very easily could have not been home. In fact she had been in Bucharest for a while filming a move. She was not the star role but had a part where they filmed her talking in the train station. They paid her the equivalent of one month's wages in Romania for 5 days work. She is so beautiful. I have several pictures of her, of course. That was the reason she wasn't attending church. I asked her if she would be going back and she said "da" (yes).

Another request Robert Vadurri had was he wanted to visit an orphanage where a special girl of his was transferred to near Teccuci. (Roxanne's home) and no one knew where it was. We asked Roxanna and she knew so she showed us where it was. At the orphanage we took lots of pictures. They love to have their pictures taken. Several cried because they thought they were being left out. One little girl asked another to have her picture mad with her and she refused – she couldn't find anyone that would take their picture with her so MY Roxanne took her by the hand and motioned for me to take their picture. She just beamed!! She hugged the both of us and I was SO PROUD of Roxanna. We asked her name and her name was also Roxanna – that really made her smile – her eyes were just glistening. It was totally awesome. I have pictures that will melt your heart. We didn't get to stay as long as we wanted to because Robert had a meeting but I realized I would never have had enough time.

Romania 2001

Another request was that I get pictures of a real shepherd and his sheep. We got a couple on the way back to Galati and Matt got some for me while we were riding the train. I want to show our kids = the kids in Romania can REALLY relate to the Good Shepherd because their neighbors and family members are shepherds.

I also got to see Nicople Church. Two years ago when I went there, I got a picture of the beginning. Dirt floor and rafters. I gave my testimony at the morning service and Stefanica asked specifically if I would some Sunday afternoon to do a children's program and I got a picture of it completed and it just blessed my heart. To see a tangible work of God's hand. Can't wait to share the pictures. Stefanica is the pastor of that church and such a very personal friend. He has a 17 year old car and even volunteered to drive us to Teccuci to the orphanage and see Roxanne. He had some sort of problems with the car on the way and stopped and asked for help and we asked if it was fixed. He said "for today". He really needs a car. I spoke with Robert because I would like to start saving money to get him a new car. We can get him a brand new car for $3,77. If anyone wants to join me, just let me know. I will talk to Mark about maybe keeping that separate from any other monies. The thing that impresses me so much is – I asked him a favor (to take us to Teccuci) and asked what time would be good for him and he said "I am your servant" I cannot tell you how much he has taught me about God's love. Two of his nephews are very special to me (Bogdon and Daniel). They have a great hero to guide their life. The Romanian translations are so loving. They are genuinely concerned when asking how are you? Bodgon Is only 14 years old – I mentioned I was ready to go back to the hotel and he said, Can I walk you there?

Such respect and insight!

Bodgon, Stephanica's nephew – a very respectful teenager

We fed this boy as he told us his dad was in an accident, bled to death and now he is the breadwinner of his home.

Redui, Romania - 2003

We started with 8 children on Sunday. On Friday we had 50 children. We had 19 salvations on Wednesday. Lots of them knew scripture from being associated with the Lord's Army and eventually join the Greek Orthodox Church. They now have a personal relationship with Christ, and their lives will be for the Lord. Many older children – 15 – 16 years old are helping the younger ones to understand this. The Pastor Tudorel and his wife are very much aware of how the children are the future of Redui. They are willing to cry with the hurting and rejoice with those who are rejoicing. They help the poor and encourage them. Redui will someday be a mighty city for God. Mihai is very supportive of the village and is confident of a great future.

Our team this year was hand-picked by God, even the translators. Each team member was looking out for one another. The leadership was awesome in walking beside George in his physical problem and in standing by Matthew in his time of grief. I sprained my ankle (minor compared to others) in Nicople on Saturday and many prayed. God was faithful. I had very little pain. I expressed my thanks to a translator named Joseph, his answer was "no thanks are necessary, it is our job". This was the attitude of the team and this is why I say it was hand-picked by God. We had a black man on our team. He lives in Kileen. He loves the Lord. He was a VIP in Redui. The people had never seen a black (Negro) man before. Everyone wanted their picture taken with him. It opened doors we could not have opened otherwise. It was an extreme blessing for me to be part of this team. The children's workers in Redui expressed to me that from my teaching the children learned a lot and yet they were so gifted I did not feel I had done much and again realized how God picked the team. Kim keeps saying I am the one who know how to teach, that's not true, we are a team that God uses at New Hope and we cannot do this ourselves. We need Him, first, then us. I am so thankful for our team at New Hope. It is not only Kim and I but also all the Sunday school teachers and Children's church workers and nursery. Workers who direct our children at New Hope in the way they should go. On Tuesday I asked the children who did not have Bibles. About 5 raised their hands. So we gave the New Testaments. I told them to go home tonight and Jean John 1:1-5. The next day I asked them if they read it and several raised their hands. I asked who understood it and couple said it was about light. One little boy raised his hand (his name is Bodgon, about 8 years old) and he stood up and quoted all 5 verses by heart. We met him in the streets while evangelizing – he was riding his bike. Under his shirt he was carrying his Bible. I have great confidence that God will do a mighty work in this town of Redui. Please pray for them. The next night I asked them to read 6-10 several read it and one other child had memorized 1-5. Seems like all they need is a little encouragement.

The 8 children of Redui with teachers at
the beginning of our week there.

The prayers from the body of New Hope were very much appreciated. I did not see Roxanna but it was because of a misunderstanding of the translator and I know God says no sometimes, wait sometimes. But actually we prayed for her to lead someone to Christ and I believe God will honor that in His time. While working with the children I realized how much I miss the service and being able to be with my family. I missed so much listening to His work because I was with the children the whole time. Somehow I would like to help those at New Hope who don't get to attend church because of their responsibilities with the children. The only way I know to do that is to volunteer so that they can.

Me and children's teacher in a field of sunflowers.

The 2007 trip was published in the *Melrose Mirror,* a local paper. That's interesting in light of the fact that nowadays you aren't supposed to talk about religion, but the editor of the *Melrose Mirror* published it anyway.

Thoughts on visiting Romania

... about children, rules and religion

from Lillian Martin

Romania is shaped like a bouquet of flowers. The Danube River comes from Germany, Austria, and Hungary and along the Yugoslav/Romanian border to Galati into the Black Sea through the Danube Delta.

Romania was the battlefield for Germany and Russia. They tried to be neutral. They lived under Ceausescu until December 1989. They were under his rule for 45 years.

Then in April 2007 Romania became a member of Europe United Community.

Our Flights from the United States:

Austin to Atlanta – 2 hours 18 minutes

Atlanta to Paris – 8 hours 15 minutes

Paris to Bucharest – 2 hours 50 minutes

Then we traveled about 4 hours to the city of Galati in a van.

Total flight time was 13 hours 23 minutes.

Return Flight

Again taking a van from Galati

Bucharest to Paris – 3 hours 10 minutes

Paris to Atlanta – 9 hours 10 minutes

Atlanta to Boston – 2 hours 42 minutes

Total flight time was 15 hours and 19 minutes.

At 37,000 feet we were going 582 miles an hour and the outside temperature was -49 degrees.

I stayed with Ulia and Marcel Maxim and their one daughter Alex, four years old. They live in an apartment building on the seventh floor, in the city of Galati. Two times while we were there the elevator actually worked, so we got plenty of exercise. She worked at a bank and he worked at the church. Breakfast was a must.

We were served a good breakfast every day we were there – consisting of meat, cheese, yogurt, juices, and fresh tomatoes and cucumbers, along with water and coffee. The coffee is very strong so you don't need much. Ulia loved to cook, when we arrived one night she had homemade ice cream made of a fruit similar to our cantaloupe, with honey. It was delicious. Another night she made a dessert that had a flaky pie crust top and it was delicious also.

Marcel is Stefanica's son. Stefanica is an awesome pastor. He takes care of four churches. One is in a village called Nicople – it is a small church with only five members that once had many. However, the population is decreasing because when the young grow up they get married and move to Italy or someplace else to make a better living, and the old folks die there.

I laughed at the message on his T-shirt in another language. I asked if that was Romanian; he said, "No it is German." He said it says:

"Shoot me – I married too young." He has been married for 38 years.

He sings praise songs all the time and his favorite he will sing for you anytime you ask – the words are from I Timothy 1:17,

"Now unto the King eternal, immortal, invisible, the only wise God be honor and glory for ever and ever. Amen."

Ulia and Marcel Maximum and daughter Alex

Redui

I was assigned to the village of Redui. The Pastor's name is Tudorel Gheorghita and his wife Flori is in charge of the children.

Our purpose is to tell them that Jesus had died for their sins and offers them the gift of heaven. We are not trying to get members in this particular church but to make sure they know how to get to Heaven. If you have any questions about our trip or our purpose, please be sure to ask me. I will be happy to talk to you.

I had visited there four years ago. When we first started the church, we had seven children and by Friday we had 60 Children. This time there were only ten children coming because the Orthodox priest in the village told them not to come and that the candy we were giving them had poison in it. The teachers of the school also told them if they came to the church, they would give them bad grades. The time we were there more came because it was not during the school year but they still feared the priest. He told the parents he would not bring communion to them or bury their families if they got involved in the church. The fear is very real.

There are lots of medical needs in the village of Redui. One mother called Tudorel (I won't try to pronounce the last name – it's difficult) and wanted prayer for her 17 year old son. When he was 1 and a half years old, the doctor gave him a shot that he had a reaction to and that stunted his growth. When we arrived she was afraid for us to go in because the priest would find out, but since we were from America we were allowed to go in. It is so sad. He just lay there, recognizing his mother and smiling and that's all he could do. We asked if we could pray, she said yes. I could only cry with the mother, telling her she is a good mother.

David laid hands on the boy and prayed for him. I stroked his forehead and he didn't flinch but I am not sure he was comfortable so I didn't do that very long. Tuderol said he had visited before years ago and the boy is the same. The mother has three other children. The two younger ones are small. She also has a 14 year old boy that likes to go to the church. The mother was confronted by the Priest and she simply told him that he is a teenager and he does what he wants to do. He thoroughly enjoys the church and would rather hang out there than with his other friends.

Mihai Dumitrascu (pastor of the mother church in Galati) made a suggestion that if the Americans could bring a medical team in the future a great number of people could be helped.

*Ana Marie who
crocheted an item just
for me. Her brother was
watching us, too.*

The children in Romania learning songs in our Bible School

We visited an organization called the Heart of a Child where they try to care for the children that have needs. They have emptied the orphanages in Bucharest and provided foster homes for the children in need. They also go into the villages to see if there are any needs there. I gave the information to Tuderol to call to see if there was anything they could do for this boy. The mother would not be as afraid because it wasn't a church helping him. (I will explain more about the Heart of a Child later in this report)

While walking the village, a little girl was sitting with her mother and grandmother and they were teaching her how to crochet. I asked if that was the first piece she had done and she said yes. I told her I would like to have something she crocheted. The next day as we were walking the village, she came up to me and handed me something wrapped in a piece of gauge. It was an item she crocheted just for me. She had also written a little message to me in English. Her name is Ana Marie. She came to church the next night and I had a bible ready for her and a box of crayons. I told her I was very happy to receive her gift and I hoped she would enjoy mine. She said she liked it very much. Her attitude was that she expected nothing in return. She was very thankful.

We visited an elderly lady who had physical problems and her husband had mental problems. I talked with her through the interpreter and asked her several times if I could pray for her. Each time she said no. She said the priest prayed for her and nothing happened. She paid the priest to pray for her. I told her I would not charge her anything to pray for her. She still said no. Finally, she did agree and I prayed for her. I prayed for not only her physical body but her emotional body and for God to take away the fear.

There are a lot of men that beat their wives in this village. We saw an older lady walking to the police station and a translator told me it was because her husband had beaten her.

It was very hot – over 100 degrees most days. They worked in the fields all day – it is very hard on them. At night they are very tired and just want to try to stay cool in the shade outside their homes. They have to get their water from a well. Most drive their wagons to the well to carry the water back to the house. They raise cows and when it is milking time the cows just walk down the middle of the street toward their homes. All the animals know the way home. Even a flock of ducks were out in a field and as we walked by, they all lined up behind each other and went directly to their home. The first one ducked his head under the fence and the rest did the same.

I was impressed that, when a man needed shoes put on his horse, he went to the man that does that in the village but when he saw that he was drunk, he told him he could not do it right now. There was no anger or harsh words, just simply you cannot do that now because you are drunk.

I have taken pictures of the children mostly because that is such a luxury. I tell them they can pick up the pictures at the church because I will send copies to the Pastor once they are developed. One lady was driving her horse to get water and she had her small child in the wagon, so I took a picture. Then she motioned to me that she would like a picture of me in the wagon next to her so I climbed in the wagon and had someone take our picture. She wanted to give me a ride but the Romanian leader I was with thought it was not best for me to do that.

Children in Romania were very pleased to see us but cautious because of the fear of the priest.

Hospital Visit

Mihaela had a friend that was in the hospital and asked if I would come with her to visit her. She said she talks like she is a Christian but she wasn't sure. She had been in a car–motorcycle accident and fractured her ribs. (She was 35 years old). We arrived at the gate and the guards would not let us in because it was not visiting hours but Mihaela knew how to get in, we simply walked through the emergency room into her room. It was a very simple room – clean with 3 beds in the room. When we arrived one lady (85 years old) was reading a Bible. We talked for a while and I asked Mihaela if it was okay to give her friend a Bible and she said yes. As it turns out the lady reading the Bible had borrowed it from Mihaela's friend so she gave the one

I gave her to the older lady. She was so thankful to have a Bible all her own. She was obviously a Christian.

The lady in the 3rd bed began to cry and we asked what was wrong. She said her doctor had told her she might not live until Thursday. We prayed for her. She has a tumor – she pointed to her lung or breast – we were not sure which she meant. I didn't have any more Bibles so I gave her a Four Spiritual Laws pamphlet in Romanian to read and she immediately began to read it. We talked to the others while she read it. After a few minutes she was weary and had to put it down but said she would finish it later. (This lady was 60 years old). As we got up to leave, she was again reading the pamphlet. She was so hungry to receive what God had for her. We decided we needed to come back the next day with a Bible for her.

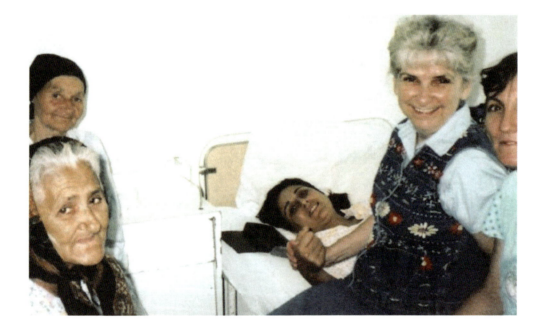

Hospital visit

The next day we visited again and she said she had read all of the pamphlet and she liked it very much. We gave her a Bible and she was very thankful also and began reading that right away. We didn't get a chance to discuss it with her but God's word does not return void. As we were visiting with the ladies, a nurse came in to tell the older lady she can go home today. (She had fallen in her yard and they were checking her out and she was fine except for some bruises).

Then another patient came in to talk with us and she was so emotionally upset she was really having a hard time while there. She had been in the hospital for 2 weeks and every day the doctor said, "We will do surgery today" and it never happened. She was young and didn't appear to be in much physical pain but she was certainly aggravated. Her husband had visited some but he had to work and it was very hard for her to be away from her family. We gave her a Bible also. She also was delighted to have one. They took the lady who had the tumor for tests and we had to leave before she got back so I don't know the outcome but I know she is seeking God and we are promised if we seek we will find.

*Stefanica's T shirt says "Shoot me, I married too young",
along with another pastor Livu*

Heart of a Child

This is an organization started by volunteers and then the government stepped in and they have grants to help children who need parents and care. Four years ago when we arrived in Bucharest we had to be very cautious because the street kids (who lived in the sewers) would pickpocket anything they could get to survive. They even stole a camera from my backpack that year and I didn't feel them do it. This year there were no kids there and we found out that this organization had taken them off the streets and given them a home with the help of volunteers and the grants from the government.

Four years ago we visited an orphanage in Tecuci and the conditions were not good at all. The orphanage is closed now. We visited one of the foster homes. There were five children in the home with a house mother and father to care for them. They were happy, getting an education and had regular counseling because of the environment they came from still affected them. They had their own individual personalities that were encouraged and they talked about their talents. The children are given several chances to obey the rules and if not they are refused. A few of the children run away in the summer and come back in the winter because they can't find places to live. Most of them soon learn that it is best to obey the rules. The murals on the walls they painted could have been done by an artist they were so good.

The Heart of a Child organization also goes into the villages to see if they can help the poor families there. This organization is in Galati, a relatively large city, but the children who live in the villages (such as Redui) do not get the opportunity to go to school unless they can live in the city during the school year and this is expensive, so some of them cannot get even a high school education. The organization is now looking for a building to house the very poor HIV kids and disabled. They need more special treatment and it is harder to find foster parents and buildings that could accommodate them. This organization also has summer camps for the kids. They were in need of volleyballs, basketballs, etc. We brought them some for their camp. It was amazing to see the difference in these kids from an orphanage to a foster home.

Pastor Mark Weaver and Pastor Mihai Dumitrascu

Roxanna

Roxanna is a special girl of mine. In 1998 she asked me how she could find God. Ever since then she has been very special to me. We have written letters and I have visited her at other times when I was in Romania. I wanted to see her this time but found out that she lives in Bucharest now. We flew into Bucharest and out of there but the times were in the early hours (3 a.m.) so it was not appropriate to see her then. She is now 21 years old. The pastor of the church in Teccui (about 45 minutes from Galati) where she grew up visited her mom and dad on my behalf before I arrived to tell her I would be there and would like to see her. He thought maybe she would come home so I could see her. It turned out that I was not able to see her this time but I gave the pastor a gift to give to her or her parents. The last picture I got from her – looked like she was rebelling a little so I mostly wanted her to know that my love for her has not changed and most importantly that God's love is unconditional. It doesn't matter what we do, God is love. That's who He is and He does not change.

October 5, 2007

I began volunteering as a SHINE counselor in Melrose while living with my brother in Reading, Massachusetts. After much training, I served the elderly clients who had questions on Medicare and Medicaid coverage. It was very rewarding to be able to help these people. Jack Beckley, the director for the Senior Center heard about my trip and suggested publication in the Melrose Mirror. I was excited to submit that to them.

Page 10

Looking Ahead • Melrose

SHINE Counseling
Get Your Health Insurance Quesitons Answered

Lillian Martin (on left), the Milano Senior Center's new certified SHINE Counselor, shows Eileen Olsen, Chairperson of the Council on Aging, the new Prescription Advantage Enrollment Application for the Sept. 15 to Nov. 15 open enrollment

Lillian will answer your health insurance-related questions every Wednesday (except Sept 6) from 11:00 AM – 2:00 PM. If you can't get to the Center, call her at 781-662-6886.

SHINE (Serving Health Information Needs of Elders) is a program of the Executive Office of Elder Affairs.

Georgie Lewis
Coordinator

Milano Senior Center
201 West Foster Street
SEPTEMBER 2006
Melrose Mirror: http://melrosemirror.media.mit.edu

(781) 662-6886

Article from Melrose Mirror volunteering as a Shine Counselor

That was very, very special. That was the first of many times that I got to tell people about how important God is and what Jesus did in my life.

I was also involved in the Bill Glass Ministries, going into prisons and talking to inmates and introducing them to Christ through a variety of speakers or just encouraging them. I learned that there are many Christians in prison—people who have just made mistakes or who have become Christians in prison, and they need that encouragement. That was the beginning of a really special part of my Christian journey.

In Recognition

Of **Lillian Martin**, as you depart from fellowship at New Hope Church to continue to serve the Lord in another place of ministry. Know how much you are loved and appreciated. Your life here has been a wonderful witness for Christ. The fruit of the Spirit is evident for all to see. As a Pastor, you are truly an asset and your life will always be productive in Christian service. To God be the glory! Great things He has done!

In the Master's Love,
Pastor Mark J. Weaver
September 25, 2005

Kayleen Rosenquist was another dear friend I met at New Hope. We started up a singles ministry, and we were on the missionary committee together. We tried to raise money for different activities of the church, and we went to Bill Glass events together.

It was like we talked about being the half of each other's brain—as if we couldn't think as straight when we were apart. When we got together, it was like one idea would come out and it would be really what we were supposed to do. Kayleen was very special in my life, as I began learning what God wanted for me. She went to Peru when I went to Romania. We were searching and bonded as we shared out experiences with each other and grew in our spiritual journey. She's a missionary in Peru now.

Even when Bobby left, I never felt unloved. A lot of times we had nothing, but it didn't matter. I always felt loved, and I was always taken care of.

At one point, I called my mother-in-law and said, "Bobby's gone. Can I come there? I have no way to feed the kids, nowhere to live." She actually said no, and I'm glad she said that, because it made me stand on my own two feet, and realize that I needed to trust God. He came through tremendously. He answered so many prayers and taught the children at the same time.

When we attended Bannockburn Baptist Church, I would go to a prayer chapel for an hour every Friday evening. The kids would watch Tommy and play with him, and I remember coming back once and my daughter coming up to the door and saying, "I know what you've been praying for." I said. "How do you know what I've been praying for?" She said, "You've been praying for refrigerator." We didn't have one—I think we might have had a small one, I can't really remember—but we needed a refrigerator. She said, "Well, I just got a call on the telephone that somebody's bringing a refrigerator over." It was God's provision.

Friend Kayleen and I getting our "crosses" from Bill Glass Ministries - after 5 events each one gets a cross

When it comes to family traditions, we didn't have other family but we had each other. Thanksgiving, Christmas and Easter were special at our house. My favorite is Thanksgiving. I liked cooking a big turkey and watching it disappear! Sometimes Thanksgiving would fall on my birthday, too. When the children got older and they had the spouses' family, I felt like, "Let's just get together whenever you can." It really doesn't matter that it be on a specific day. Once I retired and moved back to Massachusetts, most of my kids call me on holidays and that is nice.

Even while living in Massachusetts, I traveled to Texas for Mother's Day, and I spent Saturday with my son and his family and Sunday with my daughter and her two boys. It didn't really matter that it was on a certain date; they know that I like to spend time with each of them and just to be with them.

As for heirlooms and keepsakes, I already mentioned the music box I received on my brother and sister-in-law's fiftieth anniversary. I also have an embroidered Ten Commandments that my sister, Marion, embroidered, that I want to pass down to my daughter, Theresa. My brother, Junior, had a rug hanging on his wall from

Africa. Billy had been overseas, and he'd bought that rug and given it to Jean. I didn't even know he went to Africa. When Junior passed away, that rug was given to me, and that's very special to me. I want to pass that on to Aeson. In his backyard, they can see deer, and Aeson gets all excited. He and his brother, Jaron call me Grandma Lillian, even though Alisa is not my blood daughter, she's close enough to it. I have other mementos for other children, grandchildren and friends and when I know it will be a "fit", I will designate the article to them.

I have always loved deer and especially fawn. When I was growing up, I wanted to have a fawn as a pet. I told Daddy that I wanted a deer for a pet. We lived in the small town of North Reading, and he took me down to the town hall, where they explained to me what I would have to do if I kept a deer.

They said, "First, you would have to have a license, and then you would have to build an eight-foot fence, because when it got older, it would try to jump over it and go back in the wild, and if it did, it would just be killed." After that was all explained to me, I realized I should not keep a real deer. So I have compromised by decorating my house with "deer".

If anyone wants to buy me something, they know a little knick-knack of a deer or a picture of a deer will make me very pleased. I really like the Scripture, "As a deer panteth for the water, my soul pants for you." Psalm 42:1. To me they are innocent and just a very special creation of God.

I have plans to be buried next to my mom and dad in Maine, and I have a statue of two fawns lying down, and I'm in the process of putting that in the place where I will be buried.

When I was speaking with Thomas lately, I told him, "That's where I'm going to be buried. Everything's taken care of. Bubba's going to be in charge, but you'll know where you are supposed to lay me, because there will be deer there." And I said, "We don't need a name on it," and Thomas said, "Yeah, we'll need to put your name on it," so I agreed to that.

Deer are just such great creatures, and anybody who knows me know I like deer, even though I couldn't have a real one. Every grandchild has to have a stuffed Bambi. We like deer meat too. Even though we love the animal, we know God provided it for food, and I have a special recipe that Thomas is very fond of—summer sausage made with deer meat and hamburger.

When the children were growing up, I liked to have all four of the kids in portraits. No matter where we went, if everybody was together, we had to take a picture. My sister-in-law Jean, Junior's wife was like that too. Whenever I would go to Massachusetts, when all the brothers and my sister and I were together, we had to take a portrait. I don't know if I got that from Jean, but she was quite an influence on my life. As I said earlier, she was the kindest person I ever knew.

I don't think I could pick out only one person to say they get the most credit for getting me from childhood to this point. It's a combination of people. My grandmother was very influential. She's probably the bigger influence. My sister-in-law, Jean was influential too and of course my sister. Because I didn't live near family, my friends became family.

In Texas, Frank Deutsch, Pastor Mark, Alisa, Kayleen and Joyce were vital parts of my family. They are my family, just as much as my grandmother and my sister-in-law and Pop were growing up, because they were able to encourage me and to confront me when I needed to be confronted—which they did. They helped me learn or teach me what I needed to know or learn in that stage in my life.

A good friend in Massachusetts was Jimmy Govoni. While living with my brother, Jr. I wanted to buy a car and knew I would have to get a job to pay for it. I applied for a part time job as a Personal Care attendant for John Cadigan. Jimmy hired me and said he would teach me all I needed to know. I had never done this type or work before. John had been in an accident at 20 years old and could not do anything for himself and my job was to help Jimmy care for him. I talked to him and tried to make his days enjoyable. I would tell him stories from the Bible, he knew some and some he did not. I was concerned for his eternity until one day we were lifting him from his bed to his wheel chair and he was obviously in a lot of pain. He looked me in the eyes and asked me. "Do you know who Jesus is?" Wow, there was my answer. It was a moment I will never forget. I told him "Yes, and He is with you right now". I helped take care of John for several years after I bought the car and became good friends with Jimmy and his wife, Marylou. Their daughter, Sarah had a baby. She named her baby Wesley, which is my nephew Johnny's middle name and so we have been praying for him. Jimmy was concerned for Wesley since his daughter did not want to baptize him. I heard that as grandfather he could baptize him. I asked my nephew, Jimmy's wife if she had some Holy Water and she did so I gave it to Jimmy Govoni so he could baptize Wesley. He did this without telling his daughter. In my way of thinking, he promised to raise the child to know God. Jimmy died in his sleep on October 6, 2012. I will miss him.

Some of the benchmarks in my life include: graduation from high school, moving to Oklahoma to live with my sister, getting married, and of course having my children, learning to support them. Growing by teaching Sunday School and trips to Romania. Coming back home to Massachusetts and learning about my childhood also has been a tremendous blessing and insight of who I am.

After my husband left, I was left to raise the three by myself. I didn't have a job or any way to support them, so I was on welfare, but I was looking for a job. I found a job with the State of Texas as a secretary. It was only supposed to be for nine months—because I was a welfare mom, and they were trying to put them to work—but after the nine months was up, three supervisors got together and said that they would find another position for me.

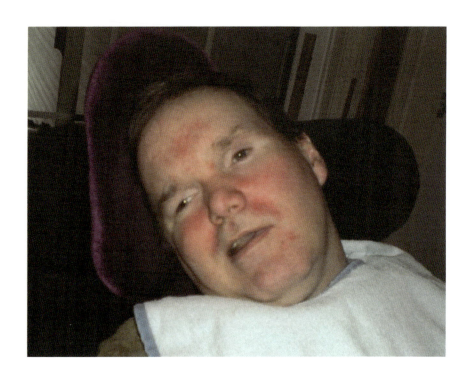

John Cadigan who I cared for here in New England

Jimmy Govoni and Aldo (Jimmy hired me to work with John and his family and I became good friends)

I had positions within the State of Texas until I retired after twenty-five years. That was an awesome provision that God gave to me, and I was able to support my children. Those supervisors also helped me find the government housing to live that was cheap, based on how much I made.

The qualifications for that job with the state were to type so many words a minute and to have one year secretarial experience. I had worked in the Alex Acosta Upholstery shop as secretary for one year before Bobby left us. It was a tremendous provision from God.

With the state job came insurance for the children. I was able to take them to the doctor— and go myself—when we needed medical care. I've retired from the state after twenty-five years, and it provides me with an income, and it also pays for my insurance. So it's obviously a blessing from God even now.

During my work for the state, computers were beginning to be used in the workplace, and as a secretary in different capacities, I learned how to operate a computer. I did that very reluctantly, but it was part of my job, and I didn't have a choice. I am extremely pleased that I did learn. Without that experience, I would not be able to even write this book or have the confidence learning new applications on the computer now.

We had to do graphs and pictures and other things. Depending on the supervisor we had, sometimes they wanted a graph of how things were going, sometimes another would say, "No, we don't need that, we just need information about the different things that we do." So I learned a variety of applications.

I remember one day when I was in the photography department, President Bush walked past my cubicle. We just said "hi" to each other. It was very interesting to see the people that came by my desk.

Another benchmark would be teaching Sunday school for fifteen years. I began teaching at Bannockburn Baptist Church because Frank knew that the director of junior church, Lillie Edwards needed some help. He asked me to help. She continued to teach me how to teach children and so I taught first grade there, then second grade at Great Hills, and then three to five year olds at New Hope. I learned so much teaching those little children. My daughter would make a cake at Christmas time for a party with "Happy Birthday, Jesus" on the top.

One co-worker, Dorothy Turner, who did the translation into Spanish of anything that we had to send out, became a special friend. She really loved the children, and she had a special place in her heart for Robert—Bubba—because she said he always seems to be full of life. He was not without getting into trouble from time to time, but he has also grown into a very responsible father. Thomas would care for Dorothy's dogs while she was away. He loved that job as she always left plenty of ice cream in the freezer.

All of my boys are awesome fathers. I am so pleased that they have turned into awesome fathers, since they didn't have one when they were growing up.

It has been awesome to see how they used their gifts in life.

When I retired from the State of Texas with 25 years of service

My Family Tree

Scotty Jay Martin
August 11, 1970

Robert Richard Martin, Jr.
December 16, 1968

Thomas Allan Martin
May 31, 1980

Theresa Ann Martin
September 16, 1967

Lillian and Robert Martin

Elwood Richardson, Sr.
Carrie Mable Connelly

Edward Martin
Theresa Poisson

Husband: Robert Richard Martin

Born:	August 11, 1946	in: Boston, MA
Married:	November 19, 1964	in: Charleston, S.C.
Died:	July 10, 2005	in: Las Vegas, Nevada
Father:	Edward Martln	
Mother:	Theresa Poisson	

Wife: Lillian Ruth Richardson

Born:	November 25, 1945	in: Winchester, MA
Died:		
Father:	Elwood Lyndon Richardson, Sr.	
Mother:	Carrie Mable Connelly	

CHILDREN:

---

1. Name: Theresa Ann Martin

	Born:	September 16, 1967	in: Charleston, S.C.
F	Married:	December 12, 1987	in: Austin, Texas
	Spouse:	Domingo Medina	

2.	Name:	Robert Richard Martin, Jr.	
	Born:	December 16, 1968	in: Summerville,S.C.
M	Married:	July 22, 1995	in: Austin, Texas
	Spouse:	Stacie Stover	

3.	Name:	Scotty Jay Martin	
	Born:	August 11, 1970	in: Summerville, S.C.
M	Married:	March 24, 2001	in: Nashville, TN
	Spouse:	Melissa Johnson	
	Other spouse:	Kathryn Megan McCalmont	

4.	Name:	Thomas Allan Martin	
	Born:	May 31, 1980 in: Austin, Texas	
M	Married:		
	Spouse:		

Theresa was the first one to leave home. She got married. She has taught in several children's day care facilities and many times was recognized as #1 teacher. She is excellent with children and the directors could not help but notice. She also worked in the nursery at New Hope.

My second child, Robert, who we call Bubba, moved out to his own apartment and eventually married Stacie Stover. He is an air conditioner repairman in Texas – no need to say he stays busy. His reputation of doing a great job keeps him busier than he wants. He wants to spend time with his children.

Scotty, my third child, entered the service right after high school graduation and made a career out of the army. He entered as a Hawk Missle Crewmember and achieved the rank of SGT in Hawk. He completed Airborne school. His duty assignments have ranged from Wildflecken, Germany to Greaves, Korea. He was deployed in support of operations in Haiti, Pakistan (Operation Enduring Freedom), Afganistan and Iraq (Operation Iraqi Freedom). He served enough years to retire but has chosen not to. He is currently working on his Master's degree.

I am very proud of him as he continues to serve our country.

I have already mentioned how proud I am of Thomas. One point stands out in his raising is what he told me when he was only 10 years old. I told him "Thomas, it would be much easier if you would listen to what I have to say and not have to do it the hard way." His answer was "Mom, you know I have to learn the hard way". That certainly was Thomas as he grew up but he is now a responsible adult and has learned how to help those who had the same attitude he had growing up.

When Thomas was the only one left living at home, and James Bouland had left, we were living in an apartment when the rent was raised $125 a month. I could not pay that and had to break my lease. At the time we were members of Great Hills Baptist Church Another member, Mr. Boyd was selling a trailer for his relative that had moved into a nursing home. I told him my dilemma and he sold the trailer for $200 a month until I paid the $2,000 for it. There was no interest charged and when I paid the total, he provided me with the title. What a provision from God – my own home!

The next benchmark after raising my children would be coming back home to Massachusetts in 2005. By then, the children had all left home. Thomas after returning from California lived with a special couple, Tom and Rowena Stenis who he called Grandma and Grampa. This is another couple in our church that was no relation but again filled a need for Thomas. I was living in a trailer that was not insulated and very hot. It was a blessing for us for a time. I could not repair it on my own. I was trying to sell it so that I could buy a one-bedroom trailer and be more comfortable, but I couldn't find one.

In the meantime, I was talking to my brother Elwood—who I call Junior. He was in his eighties. One day, I was talking to his daughter, and she made the comment that Junior had said, "Do you think she would really come home?" He sounded like he really wanted me to come home to Massachusetts.

Well, I didn't see any reason not to move. I didn't have any responsibilities in Texas, and I liked New England weather better than Texas weather. I love the fall and the spring—and even the winter snow.

I continue to enjoy the New England seasons. I spend my time outside as much as I can. Occasionally, I will sit with someone who needs temporary help but mostly I travel to see my children and grandchildren in Texas, Tennessee, Toronto and Washington. It is an awesome experience to see them grow.

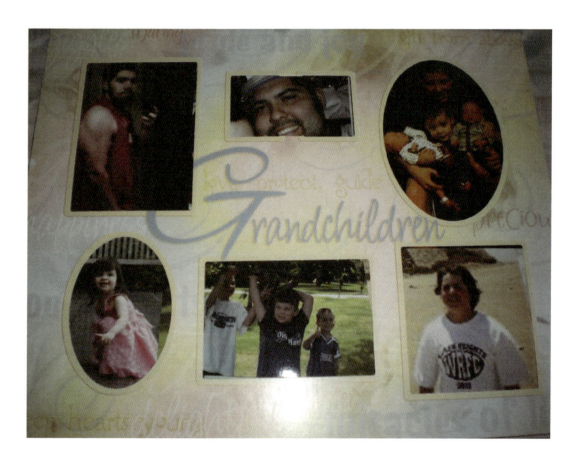

Grandchildren 2011

I sold the trailer, but I still couldn't find a one-bedroom trailer, so I said, "Well, if I can't find that, I will move back home." I did sell the trailer and, had a garage sale as I consolidated my belongings to take to Massachusetts or use in the one bedroom trailer, I realized I was in fact going back to Massachusetts. I was staying at Alisa's, and she was willing to let me remain there, but I really felt like I was supposed to go home to Massachusetts. I bought a ticket October 2005 and with belongings already mailed to my niece's home, I was on my way.

I was very surprised that my brother, Donald, said he wanted to pick me up from the airport. He was very pleased with the fact that I was coming home, and he said that he wanted to be the first one to say "Welcome home." Nice.

I lived with Junior for a while before moving into my own apartment. As I mentioned, I became a SHINE counselor while there, and then began working for Jimmy Govoni. I was finally accepted into the Housing Authority of North Reading, after being in the Reading Housing for a year. As a retired person, I pay 30 % of what I made and not responsible for repairs. That was a big load off me. Junior died in 2010 of Alzheimer's. Basically, the Alzheimer's told him not to eat. He expressed sorrow many times after Jean died of complications of diabetes and wanted to be with her. They are together now. I was very pleased that I got to spend time with him in the last years of his life especially since he had specially wanted me there.

I was living in Massachusetts for only one year when Donald and Maria's youngest daughter Lisa, who was twenty-eight years old, had an inoperable aneurism on her brain and died. It was very unexpected. She was a very talented young lady. There were no answers. Children aren't supposed to die before their parents. My brother and his wife found this poem written by Lisa that helped ease the excruciating pain. They would see her again.

Lisa Richardson - my niece who was
called home to heaven way too early

GOD WILL NEVER GO

By Lisa Richardson.

God will help me forget you, and how you don't love me anymore.

He will wipe the tears away, my heart will longer be sore.

He loves me more than I know, He will ease the pain.

Why, without Him I'd surely go insane.

He will mend my heart and sew it together.

After all, at least God is forever.

One day maybe you'll come back and love me again.

I just have to keep faith and remember God is my friend.

Through thick and thin, thicker and thinner,

God will always be there loser or winner.

Even when things seem that they are at the

worst, I won't lose hope, remember God

comes first.

So I'll dry the tears and blow the nose,

worry about my friends and not my foes.

God is my savior and my Lord, this I know.

Because in my heart I am sure, God will never go.

Then in 2009 there was still another death in the family. Junior's youngest son, Peter died of a heart attack. It also was very sudden. Junior took it very hard as anyone would when it is their youngest child. He was a very fun loving guy. I believe it took quite a toll on Junior as he passed away only five months later.

Since some people in Texas thought I went only to be with my brother, they now say, "Well, he's gone. You need to come back." But I don't feel like God's having me come back yet. I have two brothers here, and I really enjoy being in New England. They too are very dear to me.

Another big benchmark in my life was when I learned that Bobby died. He'd left us and left me to raise the kids by myself—which I did with God's help and many, many miracles in between. I didn't even know where Bobby was, but as I was trying to do the family trees, I came upon his information. I had his social security number and learned that he had died in July of 2005.

I wanted to know what he died of for medical history for his children, and through my son Bubba—Robert, Jr. — we got a copy of the death certificate, and it said that Bobby died of leukemia. He died alone in a hospice facility. The administrator of the hospice place told the coroner who he was. He was buried in the military cemetery in Las Vegas, Nevada, because he was in the navy for four years. There was no obituary.

Robert and I both said, "He knew where we were … why didn't he call us? We could have given him blood or marrow or whatever it would have taken."

Knowing Bobby, I feel like he thought he deserved what he was getting, but that's not how we felt. We only wanted grace and mercy for him. No one was with him, I had a really, really hard time over that. I didn't understand why I was so upset about his death. He had been gone for over 35 years. I would wake up crying, and I couldn't handle what was going on during the daytime.

I started going to a grief-share program from Grace Chapel, one of the churches that I attend.

I read the book *When God Becomes a Parent,* and it explained me exactly "to a 'T.'"

When God became A Parent by Darren Daugherty

It is amazing what I have learned about myself through this book.

Excerpts like –

"What does it mean to live with the loss of a parent who died in your childhood? It means that one has a constant awareness of mortality."

People think it odd how I at age 50 or so began to make all my final arrangements. Now I know why. In the back of my mind, I was more aware of my mortality than others. I remember thinking I wouldn't live past age 21.

"A part of you is always missing. Living without a mom is like being immortal but starving to death" I worried as a parent I would die sooner so at an early age I began to teach my children independence.

"One feels the absence of a parent throughout life" "You have to grieve as a child and then as an adult – your dad would never walk you down the aisle or your mother would never see your children. Those children may not miss that because they didn't experience the loss but you do."

"Children should be taught how to handle hurtful words". Evidentially I never learned that and at 65 years old, I am having an extra hard time realizing not everyone likes me and that's okay. I have always had an extra hard time in confronting anyone.

"The losses of our adult life may be compounded by the remaining unresolved losses of our childhood". I felt the loss of my husband so much that I sought out GriefShare and I am so glad I did. I see myself in a different light. I have always felt loved but the void was still there because of no mom and dad. "In childhood, the parent is not only the major loved one, she is also a part of the child's self" I had a step parent but now I know why I acted out with her so much. I didn't want anyone to take my mom's place. I know that my parents are in heaven and I will see them again but I am so thankful to God for opening my eyes to who I have become.

I will not have an adult relationship with my parent so it makes it hard to have an adult relationship with my children. I had no adolescence relationship with my parents and an extremely hard time with my children when they became adolescences.

"Samples of deceased parent's written word are among items adults value. For individuals who have grown up not knowing a parent, a parent's personal writings are a treasure." I was so excited to see a letter written by my mother to my grandmother, I shared it with my brother and it is precious to us.

"The person I became as a result of her death was a person who could be there for people who were experiencing hard times".

The blessing we seek in life is not to live without pain. It is to live so our pain has meaning.

I don't remember my mother dying. I wasn't allowed to go to my father's funeral. This book told me that I had a keener sense of mortality than others who had not gone through the experiences that I did.

I had taught my kids at a very young age that they needed to be independent and to take care of themselves, "because I'm the only one you have. There's no other family available to take care of you." I had all my funeral arrangements taken care of, and this book explained why I did that; that I was not allowed to grieve my mother's death or my father's death.

When Robert and Herbert died, there was no talk about grieving. I got to hear some of my mother's concern later, but I didn't really understand what was going on at the time. I never had a mother during my teenage years or my adult years, and it was very difficult for me to raise my children when they became teenagers and adults.

Reading that book, and going back and grieving those deaths, and looking at that made things easier for me. I stopped crying, and I was able to accept what had gone on, and now I have an awesome relationship with my adult daughter and sons. Up until that point, I was treating them like children.

When my sister died, my best friend Alisa actually taught me how to cry. She heard that my sister died, and she said, "We are going out in the public, and be prepared to cry." She took me to a Build-a-Bear, and she said, "Pick out any kind that represents your sister—to be a keepsake." I picked out a koala bear—because she had been in Brazil—and put an angel costume outfit on it, and I still have that. It's very special, and I think I began my journey of grieving for my sister through that. I didn't have that kind of help grieving all the other deaths.

The koala bear Alisa had me make when my sister died to help me grieve

Alisa and me

Bubba is an air-conditioning repairman in Texas, which keeps him very busy as I previously said. Growing up, he was always interested in taking things apart, and we had to be careful in the chairs that you sat in, because it might not be "sit able". Eventually, though, he learned how to put things back together again, and he worked at apartment complexes, repairing things. He can repair just about anything.

Bubba also liked baseball when he was growing up. He has a son now, and I'm sure the other sons as they grow will be playing baseball. Clay, thirteen, is Bubba's oldest, and he's a very good baseball player. I would not doubt at all that he could make the major leagues. I know that sounds like a grandmother talking, but I think it's true.

Theresa is an excellent gardener. She loves flowers, and can grow just about anything. One Mother's Day, she made a garden of flowers near my trailer. That was her gift for me for Mother's Day, which was very, very special to me.

Recently, I gave a friend blue bonnet seeds—they grow in Texas and not in Massachusetts— but he was able to grow two in Massachusetts, and when I went to visit Theresa, I brought them to her. She was really excited, and hopefully she can get it to grow there in Texas. Even though blue bonnets are wildflowers there in Texas, for some reason it's hard to get them started.

When Theresa had her first baby, I was very excited. The baby was very large— eleven almost twelve pounds. I waited in the hospital waiting room for quite a while, and I guess I got overly nervous, and I just walked into the delivery room.

The doctor looked up and said, "Who are you?" I said, I'm her mother," and I just walked to my daughter. Her husband was there with her, but for some reason, because that was my first grandchild, I couldn't wait the time it took

I was not happy when the doctor delivered JT and they said, "That's why you had such a hard time. He's a big one." I thought, *well, you're supposed to know that*, and so I wasn't really happy. But maybe I said more than I should have at the time. Both of Theresa's boys were good-sized when they were born. They were surely Texas sized babies.

My Family Tree

Jacob Anthony Medina
July 15, 1992

Justin Tranquilino Medina
July 22, 1988

Theresa and Domingo Medina

Robert Richard Martin, Sr.
Lillian Ruth Richardson

Domingo Medina, Sr.
Nancy Castro

JT and Jacob are in their twenties now, and Theresa has raised them very responsibly. JT was very good at football and got a scholarship and went to college part-time. I have a very special picture I took not too long ago, and they look like my bodyguards. They're very special kids. JT has two jobs now. Jacob works with his dad. They're very responsible kids.

Husband Domingo Medina, Jr.

Born:	November 30, 1963 in:
Married:	December 12, 1987
Father:	Domingo Medina, Sr.
Mother:	Nancy Castro

Wife:	Theresa Ann Martin

Born:	September 16, 1967 in: Charleston, S.C.

| Father: | Robert Richard Martin, Sr. |
| Mother: | Lillian Ruth Richardson |

CHILDREN:

1.	Name:	Justin Tranquilino Medina
M	Born:	July 22,1988 in: Austin, Texas
	Married:	
	Spouse:	

2.	Name:	Jacob Anthony Medina
	Born:	July 15,1992 in: Austin, Texas
M	Married:	
	Spouse:	

Oldest grandsons

Youngest grandsons

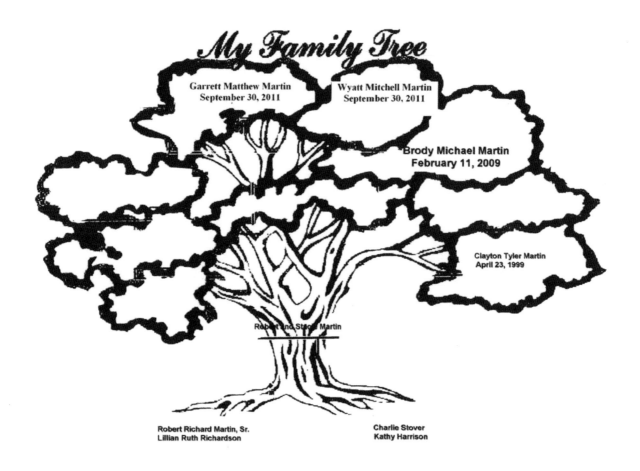

My Family Tree

Garrett Matthew Martin
September 30, 2011

Wyatt Mitchell Martin
September 30, 2011

Brody Michael Martin
February 11, 2009

Clayton Tyler Martin
April 23, 1999

Robert and Stacie Martin

Robert Richard Martin, Sr.
Lillian Ruth Richardson

Charlie Stover
Kathy Harrison

Robert's oldest, Clayton, is thirteen. He's very compassionate. Clay knows that I have a bad sense of direction – I can get lost going around the corner. So I'd go to his baseball games, and usually I'd stay at Alisa's house when I was visiting. Clay would call me to make sure I got there all right, and I'd ask Bubba, "Did you tell him to call me?" The answer was, "No. He just called himself." I see the compassion and the interest that he has for me. Tommy has that, too and so that's why Clay reminds me of Tommy. Brody is as I have said "like his dad" and very energetic, he loves to ride the train in the park when I visit. The identical twins are very young and so much fun. It is hard to tell them apart even for Bubba and Stacie.

Husband: Robert Richard Martin, Jr.

Born: December 16, 1968   in: Summerville, S.C.

Married: July 22, 1995   in: Austin, Texas

Father:	Robert Richard Martin, Sr.
Mother:	Lillian Ruth Richardson

Wife:	Stacie Michelle Stover

Born:	October 10, 1969	in: Austin, Tx
Father:	Charlie Stover	
Mother:	Kathy Harrison	

CHILDREN:

1.	Name:	Clayton Tyler Martin	
M	Born:	April 23, 1999	in: Austin, Texas
	Married:		
	Spouse:		

2.	Name:	Brody Michael Martin	
M	Born:	February 11, 2009	in: Austin, Texas
	Married:		
	Spouse:		

3.	Name:	Wyatt Mitchell Martin	
M	Born:	September 30, 2011	in: Austin, Texas
	Married:		
	Spouse:		

3.	Name:	Garrett Matthew Martin	
M	Born:	September 30, 2011	in: Austin, Texas
	Married:		
	Spouse:		

My Family Tree

Taylor Christopher Martin
October 2, 1997

Scotty and Megan Martin

Robert Richard Martin, Sr.
Lillian Ruth Richardson

Robert Des McCalmont
Valerie Joan Wheeler

Taylor lives with his mother in Toronto, Canada. He is in his teenage years right now. He is very respectful and kind to me. He is a great kid.

Husband:	Scotty Jay Martin	
Born:	August 11, 1970	in: Summerville, S.C.
Married:	February 19, 1997	in: Killeen, Texas
Father:	Robert Richard Martin, Sr.	
Mother:	Lillian Ruth Richardson	

Wife:	Kathryn Megan McCalmont	
Born:	December 14, 1967	in: Toronto, Canada

Father:	Robert Des McCalmont
Mother:	Valerie Joan Wheeler

CHILDREN:

1. Name:	Taylor Christopher Martin	
M Born:	October 2, 1997	in: Killeen, Texas
Married:		
Spouse:		
Other spouses:		

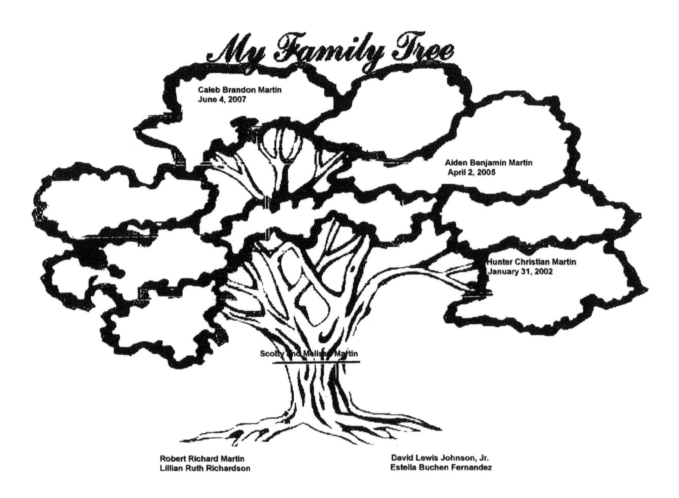

My Family Tree

Caleb Brandon Martin
June 4, 2007

Aiden Benjamin Martin
April 2, 2005

Hunter Christian Martin
January 31, 2002

Scotty and Melissa Martin

Robert Richard Martin
Lillian Ruth Richardson

David Lewis Johnson, Jr.
Estella Buchen Fernandez

Scotty's three children are home schooled and love to learn new things. Hunter loves to draw, Aiden loves to read, and Caleb is into superheroes. The family is very active in their church teaching them fundamentals of the Christian walk.

Husband: Scotty Jay Martin

Born:	August 11, 1970	in: Summerville, S.C.
Married:	March 24, 2001	in: Nashville, TN
Father:	Robert Richard Martin	
Mother:	Lillian Ruth Richardson	

Wife: Melissa Johnson

Born:	October 5, 1972	in: San Benito, Tx
Father:	David Lewis Johnson, Jr.	

Mother:	Estella Buchen Fernandez

CHILDREN:

1.	Name:	Hunter Christian Martin	
M	Born:	January 31, 2002	in: Ft. Bragg, TN
	Married:		
	Spouse:		

2.	Name:	Aiden Benjamin Martin	
M	Born:	April 2, 2005	in: Ft. Bragg, TN
	Married:		
	Spouse:		

3.	Name:	Caleb Brandon Martin	
M	Born:	June 4, 2007	in: Ft. Bragg, TN
	Married:		
	Spouse:		

My first granddaughter name is Miya. Thomas and Michelle Campbell are her parents. I have visited a couple of times when she was first born but they are separated now. He is in Seattle, Washington, and he kept me up with the birth by phone. He sent me a picture of the baby's sonogram, and we knew it was a girl.

She is a very sweet girl. They are working out visitation. Thomas is devastated that he cannot see her as much as he would like.

Father:	Thomas Martin	
Born:	May 31, 1980	in: Austin, Texas
Married:		
Father:	James Coleman (on birth certificate is Robert Martin)	
Mother:	Lillian (Richardson) Martin	
Mother:	Taeko Michelle Campbell	
Born:	January 19, 1971	
Father:		
Mother:		

CHILDREN:

1.	Name:	Miya Michelle Martin	in: Seattle, Washington
F	Born:	June 9, 2009	
	Married:		
	Spouse:		

Tommy's grandfather was a very good influence on Tommy when he was little. He had a barber shop, and he used to help me by giving all the boys haircuts. He also helped me around the house a lot. When we learned that Tommy and Michelle were going to have a baby, his grandfather's comment was that his other children had all girls, so he guessed Tommy's was a girl too. That's okay with me. I'm happy with a little granddaughter.

Bubba always had a lot of energy, and he enjoyed life, and grew up learning responsibility. When he and Stacie were going together, Stacie started college, and they would call back and forth. It was long distance. I was on a very limited income, feeding teenagers. So I got the bill, and it was $300. When Stacie came back from college, she and Bubba were sitting outside our duplex in a car, and I just walked up to him and said, "This is the telephone bill, and I can't pay it. If you don't pay it, we're not going to have a telephone." Well, he immediately went down the road, and got a job selling Christmas trees and paid back every bit of the $300 we needed for the telephone.

My twenty-fifth high school reunion was a special time for Scotty, Tommy, and me. I really wanted to go, but I didn't know if I should. I prayed about it, and I looked into going by train. When I learned that I could get my money back up until an hour before the train left, I went to the bank and asked if I could borrow that much money on my signature. They agreed, and I kept feeling like God was letting me go on the trip. I hadn't been home in twenty-five years, except to my brother's funeral.

Theresa and Bubba—Robert—were out of the house already, and Scotty had just graduated from high school. Tommy was eight. So Scotty, Tommy, and I took off, and we went to Massachusetts by Amtrak. It took two days and a night.

My brother, Donald, met us at the train station in Boston and was very, very pleased to see us. We hugged. Scotty got a little carsick on the way to New Hampshire from Boston. It's not that far, but I think it was from being on the train for so long.

When we got to Donald's house, Tommy went up to his wife and said, "You know what my mother and your husband did? They were hugging for a long time." My sister-in-law chuckled and told him that was all right. "They're brother and sister." Evidently, Tommy didn't understand or hadn't put that together yet, but it was very sweet, very cute.

I stayed with Donald for part of the time, and then I went to my reunion, and I stayed with my older brother, Junior, for part of the time. When it got time to leave, Donald gave me an envelope, and in the envelope was money that would cover the whole trip. It was like God was saying, "This is a gift from me." I think that was a miracle.

Later on, when I told Donald about it, he said, "I don't remember anything about that," but my brothers Billy, Donald and Junior had all put money in that envelope, and when I opened it, the money covered the loan and everything I needed for the trip. It was just a very special blessing from God, because I hadn't seen my family in twenty-five years.

When we returned, Scotty decided he was going into the army. I was concerned because he had not grown up with a father. A man had never even hollered at him. He did extremely well. I believe Frank was an influence since he had been in the service and was Scotty's mentor. Scotty told me after basic training that he really learned how to depend on God. I know that's a hard lesson but very worthwhile.

My faith has really grown over the years. Faith either grows or diminishes, according to how you see God and if you're listening to him, attending church or reading your Bible or taking courses.

I took one course called "Experiencing God," and it helped me learn what God wants from me. It had a great impact on my life.

God has always met me where I was at, even when my faith was small. Wherever I was at, God was there and over time, my faith got a little bit deeper. It was like stepping-stones into where I should be at this point. My faith was always growing, always alive. For example, I might read a Scripture one time and get one point, and then another time, something else would pop out at me. I believe that's because the Holy Spirit is real, and God speaks what a person needs to hear at a particular time.

The single most profound realization of my spiritual journey has been experiencing God's unconditional love, no matter what I did. God loves me. I couldn't be so bad that he wouldn't love me, and I couldn't do enough good to earn his love. His grace is enough.

I didn't have a clue how to raise children, but gave them unconditional love, and then God took over from there. Children need to have the sense—like I did—of always feeling loved. Even when I wasn't exactly doing what I should have done, that unconditional love would come from God. I think that, as parents, we need to mirror that to our children, so that they can see God's unconditional love.

I would like my children, my grandchildren, and the people whose lives that I've touched and have touched my life to know that I loved them unconditionally.

I'd also like them to know that I had a lot of trials in my life, but that's not a bad thing. Trials helped me see things. I'm a little bit stubborn sometimes, but the good side of that is perseverance. I would hope that my family and friends would see that I persevered, and I did what I needed to do—what I was directed by God to do. I didn't always follow the right path, but when I did, I felt a very special accomplishment. God used that sense of accomplishment to encourage me to keep on, and I would like them to never give up.

Never in my wildest dreams growing up did I think I would ever leave this little town of North Reading, and yet I've been all over the country and to Romania. Never in my wildest dreams did I think that I would go to Romania. I would like to encourage the next generations to keep all their options open. God may be opening a door to go somewhere or to do something that's different from what you think you can do. I certainly didn't think I would lead another person to Christ when I was fifty-three years old. I figured I should have been doing that all along, but God meets you where you're at. Be open to what you feel like he's telling you to do, and lean on him in the hard times—and don't forget him in the good times.

I think it was a miracle that I was able to raise three children without their father and without my family around. At times, we didn't have material things that we needed, and they would appear—like the refrigerator. I couldn't drive a car, and an elderly neighbor said he would teach me how. Things like that.

It's been such a pleasure to see how my children have grown into responsible adults and how they are raising their children. They're an awesome bunch of children and grandchildren. I'm very proud of the way my children have raised my grandchildren.

I would not like it any other way. They have taken the children that God's given them and accentuated the positive and encouraged them. I'm extremely proud of the men my sons have become and of my daughter who has raised two huge boys who are gentle and kind. I'm very proud of all of them.

The one thing I would say to encourage my children and grandchildren when I'm no longer around would be: recognize who you are in Christ. The Bible says to love the Lord your God with all your heart and to love your neighbor as yourself, and if we do that, we can accomplish anything. I would encourage kindness and encouragement.

I learned a lot the hard way, but I also learned a lot by encouragement. For example, when Thomas was growing up, I could give him encouragement, and it would last a long time. But if I had to criticize or say something negative, then it would crush him. Encouragement is the way to go.

Encourage each other, your children, and your grandchildren. I'm hoping that the events that are hard to read about in my book—what I went through—I hope that they would be an encouragement that no matter what they go through, they can make it.

I've included a "charge to next generation" in this story. My mother was a strong Christian, my grandmother was a strong Christian, and I tried to do what God told me to do. So my charge to the next generation is to keep the faith no matter what happens.

Charge to the next generation

(Theresa, Robert (Bubba), Scotty and Thomas)

"You will face mountains so steep, deserts so long and valleys so deep. Sometimes the journey's gentle, sometimes the cold winds blow. But I want you to know you will never walk alone…Jesus will be right beside you all the way" He'll walk alongside us and hold our hand at the "scary" parts. -Anne Cetas

Keep the faith that dwelt first in your great-grandmother, Lolie and your grandmother, Carrie and now dwells in you. And with your mom, Lillian, who struggled to stay on the path God wanted for me. My belief was strong as I always knew God loved me, however, I did not always walk straight but always obtained Mercy and Forgiveness.

(Borrowed from 2 Timothy 1:5)

Ten Commandments – Deuteronomy 5:6-21

Fear the Lord your God, you and your son/daughter and your son's/daughter's son/daughter by keeping His commandments. Deuteronomy 6:2

My favorite verse is 1 Corinthians 10:13 There hath no temptation taken you but such as is common to man but God is faithful who will not suffer you to be tempted above that ye are able but with the temptation also make a way to escape that ye may be able to bear it.

And I found even when I chose to succumb to temptation that: If we confess our sins, He is faithful and just to forgive us our sins and to cleanse us from all unrighteousness. 1 John 1:9

You shall teach them diligently to your children and talk to them when you sit in your house and when you walk by the way, and when you lie down and when you rise. Deuteronomy 6:7

And you shall write them on the doorposts of your house and in your gates. Deuteronomy 6:9

Theresa using her gift s and reminds us to smile

One of the reasons I wanted to write the book was to give my children a glimpse of where they have come from and say that even though we went through some really tough times, God was always there. Sometimes you really don't feel like He is there, but He's always there. So keep the faith. Realize that you have not been abandoned and that no matter what happens, God loves you. Keep the faith. As you teach my grandchildren and great-grandchildren, carry on the generation of Christian ethics that we believe. We're not perfect, but we follow Christ.

The most vital thing that I would tell my children and grandchildren is to keep on keepin' on. Never give up.

Never give up

Made in the USA
Charleston, SC
24 November 2013